To SAVE ONE Child

THE AUTOBIOGRAPHY OF
G. WALTER ERICKSON, M.D.

TO SAVE ONE CHILD
G. Walter Erickson, M.D.

For information address:
G. Walter Erickson, M.D.
1512 S. Lake George Drive
Mishawaka, IN. 46544

First Edition published 2003.

© 2003 G. Walter Erickson, M.D.

Cover & Book Design:
BigHead Studios

A collaborative publication of:
Gold Leaf Press
33 Crocker Blvd.
Mt. Clemens, MI 48043

1098765432

ISBN 1-886769-27-3
Soft Cover; 202 pages
$17.95

DEDICATION

This book is dedicated to all the nurses with whom I have been privileged to work during the past 50 years. Two specific groups of hospital staff nurses were outstanding in their ability and devotion to their patients.

The first were those nurses who worked at Northern Indiana Children's Hospital during the polio years of 1950 to 1955. They were: Dorothy Mitchell, Joanne Linster, Carolyn Ushela, Betty Pinter, Julia Street, Lucy Sacks, Hester Matthews and Ruth Tulchinsky. There was one outstanding aide, Marie Scott, who mothered all the nurses and doctors.

The second group was the pediatric nurses of Memorial Hospital who worked during 1960 to 1980. These were: Connie Guerra, Debbie Hibschman, Cheryl Laskowski, Roxanne Ewing, Kathy Van Lue, Eileen Whitten, Kathleen Klawitter and Marian McQuade. Ruth Jackson was an outstanding aide.

TABLE OF CONTENTS

ACKNOWLEDGEMENTS

My book could not have been completed without the computer knowledge and encouragement of Martha Lake Adams Erickson, my wife for 57 years.

I wish to thank my children, Garwood Elliott, Robin Erickson Gebrian and Quincy Erickson, the jewels of my life. Each one of my children have grown up to be mature independent thinkers who are involved in their communities and are making a difference in their worlds.

I wish to thank all the parents of my patients who granted me the honor and privilege of helping to raise their children in sickness and in health.

INTRODUCTION

What have I learned from 50 years of practicing and teaching Pediatrics to doctors, nurses, parents and children?

I have learned that a child needs two parents. Many of my never married or divorced mothers live in poverty and despair.

Too many young women have no understanding of how to choose a husband. Even if they select a suitable man, most wives have no clue how to retain him.

The saddest words I heard in my office were: "My husband wants a divorce." Most wives had no knowledge that anything was wrong with their marriage.

The other sad words were: "My husband had a heart attack."

How inadequate it is to offer words of sympathy when a divorce or death occurs. It is far better to provide anticipatory guidance and try to prevent these catastrophes.

Teaching young ladies how to choose a husband should be part of proper Pediatric care. Teaching wives how to maintain a marriage is as important as advice about proper care of their children.

I taught the mothers that the most important thing they can do for their children and themselves is to maintain their marriage. That includes looking after the health of their children, their husband and themselves.

Advice to mothers about how to be a good caretaker to their children is very simple. Know what to expect at each age and then expect it.

As doctors we can be kind and be available. We are not the star of the show. We are bit players in the great drama of life and death. We should be thankful that we have the knowledge and skill to save lives. I think that to be needed and to be able to help others is the real secret of living.

Life is almost all anticipation and reminiscence. The actual experience is fleeting.

Enjoy the journey.

G. WALTER ERICKSON, M.D.

G. Walter Erickson, M.D., in his office – 1991

1. MY STORY

I began writing my story 3 days after my 20th birthday. It was an attempt to look back in review upon my life—its first third in which I was taught and learned. Now it is 131 days after my 80th birthday and I begin my writing again.

It is not as if I did no writing between these two dates of my life. On the first attempt I wrote 100 pages and then many individual essays in between. Today, I have gathered together the dusty and faded pages and will present a chronological and analytical story of my life beginning with my formative years.

My father's parents came to America from a village near Stockholm, Sweden to find work. They settled in Middleboro, Massachusetts and became farmers. They had 13 children. My father and his brothers worked hard from sun up to sun down, sawing down and chopping up trees, clearing the land, taking the stones and making stone walls. He learned how to plant, how to cultivate and how to build.

Because there were so many children in the family, my father was farmed out until he was 5 years old to some relatives named Anderson who had no children of their own.

Education was very important in his family. All the children went to school. In the front parlor was a complete 5 foot book shelf of Harvard classics which was well read. When my father finished high school he married my mother and moved to Springfield to work in a factory. My mother encouraged my father to go to college which he did after I was born.

My mother's parents, McWilliams, came from Scotland and Ireland. They came to America because there was not enough food in their original countries. They settled in Enfield, New Hampshire. My mother was valedictorian of her class at Enfield High School but although she wanted to go to college, she didn't because she married and then had me. However, she worked in the Water Department of the City of Springfield until her forced retirement at age 65. Retiring from her job left a void in her life for the next 32 years. I was named after my father who was named after Gustaf, the King of Sweden. Many Swedish families named a son after the king.

When I was very little we lived on the first floor of a wooden tenement house at the corner of Clifton Avenue and Central Street. My father worked at the Westinghouse plant and every morning he left for work on the 5 AM trolley that went by 20 feet from our front window. My mother made his lunch and kissed him goodbye. He waited inside until the trolley came in sight from Watershops Pond and ran out to jump on. My mother and I sat on a big trunk between the front bedroom windows and waved good-bye. In the evening we were waiting there when he came home at 6 PM.

Our tenement house had an inner courtyard with back porches. This was the social and play area for all four floors. It was where my mother's square clothes rack held our drying clothes on washdays—weather permitting.

My father made a toy box for me that we kept on the back porch. It was the most wonderful thing ever built. In it were all my worldly possessions. A car stuck out this way, a trumpet that way. I never knew what forgotten treasure I would find when I pulled out something as everything shifted position. Later my father built a swing on the porch that made me the envy of all the neighborhood children. Our prime goal was to swing high enough to touch the bathroom window. I was king of the tenement until a disrupting influence arrived.

Barbara came to live in the tenement apartment next to ours. Barbara was beautiful. Her tea parties attracted all the boys away from my back porch and my swing and the feud began. She would serve tea on her porch while I, uninvited, watched alone from mine. One summer night it was very hot and my mother made some lemonade. Barbara heard the clink of the glasses and looked over the porch rail. "Why don't you invite Barbara over?" my mother asked. I weakened and opened our gate to let Barbara through.

After the lemonade was drunk, during which process we eyed one another, I asked, "Want to see my toys?" I held my favorite trolley car out to her. We pulled out all my toys and became friendlier. The next night she invited me over. Her grandmother opened the porch icebox and took out ears of corn. We sat on the edge of the porch and ate. I can still remember those summer nights on the back porch eating ears of corn sprinkled with salt and pepper and smeared with butter as the street lights came on.

One day in August a family moved into a house next door. The first I knew that someone was there was the sight of two ragged, somewhat dirty children who eyed us over the fence. At noontime, after venturing no closer than watching, the two children went inside to eat. About 1:30 PM we heard the sound of music. "A band. Come on." All of us ran down the street. There was no band but we still heard the music. At the door of a commercial garage, half in and half out, were 7 or 8 people playing musical instruments. Two of the players were the two boys who had been watching us. One played a fife and the other held a bass drum. The workers in a nearby garage came out to listen and a dozen other people gathered around. After playing a few numbers, the smallest boy who played the fife, walked around with his hat. Most of the men put some money in the hat. Then the band played some more.

Between numbers the listeners talked to the musicians. "Are you all one family?" "Do you all play?" "Is this what you do for a living?" The answer to all the questions was "Yes".

This was my first contact with children who worked. Many children began working in the mills at an early age and did not go to school but I did not know them.

I did talk to the children. They seemed older and didn't seem interested in our games. Every time we started to play, their mother or someone would call them in to practice.

Ten days after the family arrived, they left in a big touring car which they owned, instruments and all. The car would not start and had to be pushed down the street. The trolley car came along about that time adding to the confusion. The older boys got out of their car and men from the garage helped push the car to the top of the hill. It rolled down the hill and that was the last we ever saw of them.

Barbara moved away. But two houses around the corner lived a girl who was a year younger than me. I often played at her house. Her mother did not mind if we upset the whole house—and often we did. Our favorite game was to put all the furniture in one room in a big pile, sit on top and pretend that we were sailors on our ship. We sailed around the world many times.

In back of our tenement lived the Mannings, a typical Irish family made up of a hard working father, a worn-out mother, an alcoholic uncle, two older sisters, a younger one and a son my age. We played "Run Sheep Run", "Duck on the Rock", "Hide and Seek" and baseball in the street. We also had water pistol fights after a fashion but I never owned a water pistol. They shot and I dodged. We also had fistfights with me against the Manning boys and his younger sister. I was small and always lost.

What we called our front yard was 30 feet long and 8 feet wide and entirely without grass. It was surrounded by a one foot high pipe fence. Every evening we gathered there to sit on the fence and play marbles. We drew a large round circle or a small fish-shaped ring in the sand. We never had enough money to buy any marbles and we never seemed to lose too many to each other but each of us owned one Moonie or more, worth 20 or 30 cents. The moonies were our prized possession and our good luck charm. How unhappy I was when my mother rapped on the front window to indicate it was my bedtime. It hurt to go in so early while it was still light and to see the others still playing outside while I prepared for bed.

One evening the tenement janitor told us that we could not play in the front yard any more because we were making too much noise. My mother came to our rescue "If you think that you are going to deprive them of the only place they have to play, we'll move." The janitor compromised by saying that we could play if I were there.

I owned a tricycle. As the only child in the neighborhood to possess one, I was the envy of the others. Proudly I rode it. Every Memorial Day my father wove red, white and blue crepe paper around the spokes of my wheels. The final touch was an American flag for my handlebars.

FOURTH OF JULY

I did not decorate my tricycle for the 4th of July. Fireworks were more important. For weeks ahead I planned what I would purchase as more fireworks stores displayed their wares. Finally, two days before the 4th my father and I went to the store. I selected and bought about one dollar's worth of fireworks. Included was a cap gun, which I could fire before the Fourth. Upon reaching home I would sort over my purchases until my mother would say, "Be careful. Something is going to go off."

The Fourth of July was almost as important as Christmas. Every child in every state bought fireworks. Many children were burned or injured. There were almost no restrictions on what type of fireworks could be bought or used. Cherry bombs were placed under cans and when lit sent the cans hundreds of feet in the air.

The night before the Fourth I could hardly wait. I laid awake most of the night and arose at 6 AM. We gathered with the other children and took turns shooting off our fireworks. There was a family rule that everything had to be used by nightfall. Even if I had only a roll of caps left over, I could not use them after the Fourth.

Usually on July 4th night we would take the trolley to Forest Park to watch the fireworks display. I had never seen such an outstanding spectacle. There I stood, half asleep, watching bombs and the skyrockets burst while I hurried to finish my pistol caps before we went home. The people left the park by car, walked and like us, hurried to catch the trolley. Firecrackers went off underfoot. Policemen tried to keep order as individuals let loose that one last blast before another Fourth ended.

SILENT MOVIES

My earliest recollection is of having my picture taken on a Sunday afternoon. My mother and father liked the movies. Silent though they were, the movies were the best and least expensive form of entertainment available. Every Saturday night they went and often took me along but I remember very little of the shows. Usually I fell asleep on the way home.

One Saturday night my parents decided not to take me. They said, "You are to stay at home and outside until we come home". Staying out was enough to compensate for not seeing a movie. I was happy as I waved goodbye from my tricycle.

Two hours of riding up and down the neighborhood weren't bad but when the streetlights began to go on, I was scared and tired and wished my parents would hurry and come home. When the gaslights blew out it was very dark. But as soon as my parents arrived, I made a beeline for my bed and fell asleep in a second.

Being left outside was safer than being left inside. Outside there were no cars or trucks, many friendly neighbors and wide safe yards in which to play. Inside were gas stoves and lights and no one to watch over you. Baby sitters had not yet been discovered.

THE GRASS IS ALWAYS GREENER ON THE OTHER SIDE.

My world consisted of the several houses near our apartment. A street, to me, was a boundary that was not meant to be crossed. Other children my age could go to that forbidden land "across". The more they talked, the greener the grass looked over there. One sunny afternoon, I had explored every square inch of my world and found it boring. Watching the other kids cross the street to the schoolyard became a big temptation. I went down the sidewalk a block away and ran quickly across the street to join the other children.

The plan was to go see Mr. Dodge's horses. Mr. Dodge was the milkman and he kept his horses in an old stable. At first we were content with just watching the horses. Then someone said, "Let's make them move." We began throwing stones. The horses kicked against the stalls. Mr. Dodge came running out of his house. We ran and hid in the schoolyard. Before long we were all captured and brought before Mr. Dodge. "If you don't tell your parents about this, I'll tell them myself and it will be all the worse." After a further lecture he let us go.

It was late. My parents were already home. "Where have you been?" I couldn't tell them about the horses. "Across the street." The punishment: "No supper and no going out to play tonight"

I stood behind the front bedroom window and watched my friends playing marbles. Some of them had been throwing stones with me. It seemed unfair.

2. CROWDED APARTMENT

Jennie was my mother's sister. Often I heard my parents talking about her. One day we dressed up and went to a section of town where I had never been before. We walked to the top floor of an old building and knocked on the door. Jennie opened the door. She looked tired and had a baby in her arms. My mother looked around the apartment. There was little furniture. The baby's bottle was heating in a pan of water on the stove.

"Jennie," my mother said, "You are going home with us." "But, Mabelle," she started to protest but already my mother had begun picking up clothes and blankets. My mother wrapped the baby, shut off the gas stove and we left. My father protested. "We don't have room enough for her and her baby," he said. But he could see the baby was not well. Unfortunately, the baby became worse and within a month the baby died. I don't know if Jennie's husband came to the funeral. I never heard anyone speak about him.

My mother's parents came to live with us. I don't remember when or why they did but it was probably to care for me since both of my parents and Jennie worked. It was customary when I was a child for several generations to live under one roof. There were very few Nursing or Retirement Homes and there was no welfare. Each family took care of all of its members.

My grandfather Mac Williams was crippled. The doctors did not know the cause and gradually he became worse. He never had crutches or a wheelchair but he could drag himself around by clinging to the furniture. I never heard him complain. He played checkers like a champion and taught me enough tricks so that I could beat any child in the neighborhood. He told wonderful stories. I sat beside him on the couch for hours and listened. However, my mother did not always approve of his choice of subjects.

My maternal grandmother was a Quigley whose Catholic parents came from Ireland. She cooked and cleaned and watched over me. She made pies and cakes and let me lick the pans. If I was bad she threatened to tell my father who might give me a spanking. But she usually forgot to tell him.

DOROTHY

One day my mother went away to the hospital so I was told. I asked, "What's the matter?" You are going to have a baby brother or sister," my father said.

My mother was gone for two weeks. I was allowed to visit her once. She occupied a room with another woman. "Where is the baby? Is it a boy?" I asked. My mother whispered, "It's a girl, dear. You have a baby sister. The other woman had a baby too but her baby died. You must not speak about her."

Then the nurse brought in my sister. She was crying and I looked out the window in disgust. The other woman had tears running down her cheeks.

A few days later we went to the hospital again. This time my mother was dressed and the baby was with her. We went downstairs to a taxi and climbed into the back seat. "What's her name? Where is she going to stay?" "Her name is Dorothy Mae," my father answered, "and she is going to stay in our room until we find another place to live". Sure enough we went to look at another place.

NEW HOME

After our apartment, the house we found seemed very large. Then, my father announced, "We're going to move" and we were on our way. The house was only two blocks away. I moved some of my toys in my cart. Our house cost $3500 with a big mortgage. At one point during the depression, the bank threatened to foreclose but it never did.

There was plenty of space for all of us. There were two bedrooms up, one bedroom down with a living room, dining room, kitchen, big pantry, small bathroom and a back kitchen where the ice box and wash tubs were kept.

In addition to the main house there was a shed and a 4-car garage. The garage had a dirt floor and big wide doors. Since we did not own a car, my father rented each garage for $2.00 a month. He also had space for a workbench and some tools.

My grandparents occupied the bedroom downstairs. My aunt Jennie slept on a couch in the dining room. My parents slept in one bedroom upstairs and Dorothy and I slept in the other.

As Dorothy grew we became inseparable. Occasionally, I got into trouble for which I received a spanking out in the shed. One time, Dorothy protested, "You can't spank my brother." If I was dragged away, she stood at the shed door and cried. She probably saved me many a spanking.

Every Saturday was washday and the washing took all day. The water had to be heated on the kitchen stove. The clothes were washed by hand in one sink and rinsed in the other. The clothes were put through a hand wringer to squeeze as much water out as possible before they were hung to dry inside the back kitchen in the winter and outside in the summer

The kitchen stove was fueled by coal or wood. Later we had gas burners. The pantry was as large as the kitchen. Among other items stored there was one bottle of whiskey. It was never opened during my childhood and was saved for medicinal purposes only.

The cellar was only 6 feet deep with a dirt floor. The coal furnace required constant attendance in the winter. We were always either too hot or too cold. The coal was stored in a bin within easy reach of the furnace. All in all the cellar was a dirty uninviting place.

We lived south of Six Corners. The area north of Six Corners was a more rowdy lower class neighborhood that was to be avoided. This was the perception that we had, perhaps unfounded. Our area of the city was certainly not upper class but the houses were painted and the lawns were mowed and most importantly we children felt safe. It was a good place to live.

MY FATHER

Every Saturday night my father served baked beans. He soaked the beans overnight on Friday, added molasses, salt pork and other ingredients and baked them slowly in a big pot. With a loaf of brown bread from Mr. Patrell's bakery, we had a delicious meal.

Every summer my father made root beer. I don't remember the ingredients but I do remember that he used the bathtub as his mixing bowl. The root beer was then poured into large quart bottles that were topped with elaborate caps. The bottles were set aside to mature. Sometimes the pressure within the bottles became so great that a minor explosion occurred. It might seem like a lot of work to produce the root beer but there were no aluminum cans or 2-liter bottles of pop. The only drink we had otherwise was Moxie which was a black bitter concoction of unknown origin.

During the seven years it took him to complete his degree in Accounting at Northeastern University, my father worked during the day as a gun stock maker at the Watershops Division of the Armory where they made the famous Springfield rifle. He then took a position in the Auditor's Office of the City of Springfield. The first stock he ever owned was the American Motion Picture Corporation. We were a family on our way up. It was 1929.

For entertainment we had a Victrola and a few records played over and over again. My first radio was a crystal set that had a small needlepoint which had to be carefully placed on a crystal to receive sound through ear phones. Later we had a regular AM radio in a console. Our favorite programs were Amos and Andy, Death Valley Days and the Lone Ranger.

My father excelled in three areas. He could grow flowers, build projects of wood, and play a trombone and a harmonica.

Every time I plant a bush or dig in the soil or smell lilacs I think of my father. He filled our front yard and the yard next door with all kinds of flowers including Rose bushes, Tulips and Lily of the Valley and a big Lilac bush by the dining room window.

He was an excellent carpenter. He made gliders, tables, and dollhouses and fixed any wood object that needed repair in and around the house. He painted the house. He made dollhouses so big that Dorothy could play inside of them. He made a double swing set for our back porch and a doghouse for a wire-haired fox terrier who was my dog in later years.

He was very musical. He played the trombone in a marching band and in a jazz orchestra. He could play any tune requested on various harmonicas. I don't believe he ever had a music lesson.

My aunt Jennie and my father went to work each morning. My grandfather sat outdoors in the sunshine. My mother kept busy with the house and Dorothy. I attended the just finished Elias Brookings School across the street.

3. CHRISTMAS AND VACATION

Christmas was the really big holiday. The tree was selected several days before December 25th but was never brought inside or decorated until Christmas Eve. Then we strung strings of various colored lights, tinsel, red and green garlands and glass balls that we saved from year to year.

After the tree was trimmed, we placed some presents under the tree and hung our stockings, We went to bed but not to sleep because we were too excited thinking about what Santa Claus would bring us.

One Christmas morning an accident ruined our day. As always, I arose early to make sure that Santa Claus had not forgotten me. Already I had gone through my stocking—left as usual at the foot of my bed. I gathered my group of stocking treats and, still in my pajamas, came to the kitchen breakfast table. I started to sit down as my mother was pouring coffee. Excited, I jumped up and a stream of scalding coffee poured down on my right arm from shoulder to wrist. Even my presents couldn't distract me from the hurt. I remember the instant pain, the smell of the burn ointment and my refusal to let the doctor prick the blisters. The burns took 5 weeks of dressing changes before they healed. I still have an elbow scar to remind me.

This experience of my burn created an interest in learning all I could about burns when I became a doctor. I could relate to the pain and fear that my burned patients had.

The best Christmas was when I was 9 years old. The night was crisp and cold. It had snowed during the day but the long front walk had been cleared. Just as we were ready for bed, Mr. Speight, my father's boss, drove up to our front door. He brought a silver flashlight for me and a doll for my sister. The doll had a white face on one end and when you turned her upside down, she had a black face on the other. With the doll was a framed poem.

"Little girl so roguish   *And when duty calls you*
Little girl so gay   *May you do your part*
May the years all hold for you   *Just as eagerly and well*
Time to romp and play   *Bless your little heart"*

VACATION

Summer time was vacation time. I was off from school and my parents were off from work for one to two weeks. We had two standard vacations. We either went to my father's childhood home in Middleboro, Massachusetts or we went to a boarding house along the North Shore.

The standard Middleboro trip was as follows: We rode the train to Boston and changed to a train to Middleboro. Then we walked 5 miles to the farm with my father carrying me and later my sister or the suitcases. In later years someone on the farm had a car and picked us up at the train station. The huge farmhouse was built in the 1700's. In addition to my father's parents, several of his siblings lived on the farm. There was John who was a YMCA secretary, Hulda with her truck driver husband, Al, and their 3 children and Annie. Another brother, Victor, lived a field away.

Of the 12 of my father's siblings, my favorite was Annie who never married and was Head of the Math Department at Middleboro High School almost all of her adult life. The High School Yearbook was often dedicated to her and at her death a scholarship was established in her memory.

The farmhouse had bedrooms everywhere to house 13 children in the family, although two died in their infancy, one with diphtheria, the other with diarrhea. Even with all the bedrooms my father told us he had to share a bed with two or three other brothers. He never knew what it was like to have his own bed until he married. The house had a 3-holer toilet facility at the end of a corridor off the kitchen.

No liquor or playing cards were allowed in the house. The front parlor, which was seldom used, had an organ and the Harvard 5-foot shelf of classics (which were well read). My Uncle John spent much time listening to the news and stock market reports on the radio. Annie and John were both physical fitness enthusiasts and spent more nights sleeping outside than inside.

The fields were full of apple trees and all sorts of growing vegetables. There were chickens in the yard and in the hen house. The large dining room table was always filled with enough food harvested from the farm to feed a dozen people. Here we learned to like "hardtack", a Swedish circular hard rye cracker as large as an old 33 record with a hole in the center. With butter it was delicious.

There was hay in the barn but I don't remember any cows or horses. There was a dirt road out front and a pine forest in the back. The fields were bounded by stone fences erected many years ago by my father and his brothers as they cleared the fields. We walked through a cow pasture to the pond when we needed to cool off or take a bath. When the family acquired a car we drove to Duxbury to White Horse Beach. We cooked hamburgers on the beach, ate corn on the cob, whole tomatoes and tons of other foods. The water was cold but the sun was hot. A sunburn was an inevitable result of our beach excursions.

Back at the farm, we camped out overnight. We fished in the brook. We shot 22-rifles in the forest (under strict supervision). On Sundays, we went to the church at the end of Wood Street and some evenings to Fairs in town. We played all kinds of games with our many boy and girl cousins. Croquet was a permanent fixture on the front lawn. Because we had such a wonderful time at the farm, we never wanted to go home. However, one time it wasn't fun. I developed hives from eating fish and to this day cannot eat them.

This is another example of a childhood experience being father to a lifelong interest in hives and other allergic diseases.

The other standard vacation was to go to a boarding house in Salem, Magnolia or Gloucester. Our family occupied 1 or 2 rooms usually across from or near a beach. We ate all our meals at the house with the other guests. The boarding house vacations were not as much fun as the farm.

In the summer of my tenth birthday we four went to Magnolia on the North Shore where we stayed at a small boarding house. The food was very good. The sandy beach was only minutes away. Sometimes the fog rolled in from the sea so thick and damp it covered everything.

We climbed all over the rocks and the high cliffs. We saw the famous rock where the Hispanola had been wrecked. We watched the sailboat races.

One day we took the bus to Gloucester. We saw the old ships and the stack of barrels ready for burning on the night of the Cape Ann celebration. Dorothy and I had our picture taken at the statue commemorating those who go down to the sea in ships.

In the middle of this vacation we received a telegram. My grandfather Erickson in Middleboro had died. We packed our bags and left for the funeral. It was a warm August afternoon. Automobiles of the guests covered three fields around the farm. Finally, everyone drifted inside the house for the services. Dorothy and I, playing in the backyard, were the only ones left outside. "You don't have to come in," my mother said. "You take care of Dorothy."

I did very well until my sister had to go to the bathroom. I opened the back door cautiously to summon my mother but I could not find her in the group. Ordinarily my sister could use a toilet seat effectively but this one on the farm was high and precarious. I managed the situation but when it was over, I breathed a sigh of relief.

We went back to Springfield. Although we had an ice box (not a refrigerator), the food did not keep too well. So each Sunday morning I was sent to the butcher shop to pick up the meat for the Sunday dinner.

Our bread and bake goods came from Mr. Patrell's bakery which was only 2 doors away. At the end of any weekday if he had any unsold doughnuts, he blew a whistle. For 3 cents you could buy a whole bag of plain and jelly doughnuts. We kids came running and sat on the bakery steps devouring the doughnuts. Some Sunday mornings he called our house and invited me to come to the back door of the bakery to pick up a pie or cake. Mr. Patrell was a very kind man.

4. DOROTHY

Saturday afternoons I often went to the movies. They were silent, of course, but the theatres usually had a double feature that cost a quarter. One particular Saturday my cousin invited me to go to the movies with his grandfather and him. I ran upstairs to ask permission from my mother. I paused on the stairs. My mother was inside our room sitting in the old rocker. My father stood beside her. My sister who had been ill since Monday lay on my bed. She had two pillows under her head. I asked my parents "May I go to the movies with Uncle Nick?". My mother didn't answer but my father said, "All right, but don't be too late." I jumped happily down the stairs.

The movies were good and long. When they were over we walked up the hill to the Oaks Hotel where a distant relative was the chef. It was too late to get a meal but they gave us some apple fritters. George and Uncle Nick talked on and on. I was nervous. "Perhaps I'd better phone my mother," I said. "Never mind," said Uncle Nick. "We're going right now." We said good night and walked down Hancock Street toward home. The streetlights were on and a slight breeze had sprung up.

As we came within sight of home, I could see lights on in the living room. "We must have company," I said. I went around the fence and in the back door to the kitchen. My father opened the door at the bottom of the back stairs at that moment. His look scared me. "What's the matter?" I asked. He looked at me for a few seconds. Then he spoke: "Dorothy is dead." "Where's Mom," I asked. "Upstairs," my father said. "She's lying down now. You find a book to read."

I walked across the kitchen into the dining room to get a book I had started. As I passed the door, I could see my aunt and other people in the living room. They were talking and the women were crying.

I found my book, "Jerry Todd and the Talking Frog." I sat down in the kitchen to read my book and started crying. My father had been watching me. "It's all right," my father said. "We'll have to be brave for your mother's sake." I asked, "But why did she have to die?" I was heartbroken.

My uncle came from Middleboro. He wanted to phone the relatives to notify them of my sister's death so we walked to a dormitory at Springfield College where he had gone to school.

I don't remember where I slept that night. The next day I lived miserably and entirely by myself. My mother stayed upstairs in her room. Downstairs my grandparents cried continuously. Visitors came and went.

My grandfather who was crippled said that he would have crawled up the stairs to see Dorothy if he had known that she was dying.

The kitchen table was covered with food, mostly pies and cakes sent over from Mr. Patrell, the baker. Whenever I was hungry I ate something. I sat at the kitchen table. No one bothered me or saw me grieving. Now and then my mother came downstairs to greet some guest. She looked tired and she never stayed long or talked to me.

In the afternoon I saw the mailman stop at the door and drop "The American Boy" on the doormat. I ran to the door. "Why didn't you ring?" I asked. "I didn't want to disturb anyone." he said. Eagerly I grabbed the magazine and sought refuge in the new world of the magazine.

The funeral was the next day in our house. The undertaker placed folding chairs all over the living and dining rooms. The coffin was in the living room in the far corner where we always had the Christmas tree.

Flowers came until the room was covered. Their smell was overwhelming. About 2 PM the guests began arriving. They each went to the coffin and gave me a glance or a word. At 2:40 PM the minister came and my mother and father took seats at the front of the room. I sat slightly behind them with my cousin John.

Mr. Stevenson was the minister from the Asbury First Methodist Episcopal Church. He read from the Bible and read a poem which made my cry.

> *"She's yours now and since I can't have her back,*
> *I want to tell you certain things to do;*
> *Put "Mother Goose" upon the nearest shelf*
> *And keep a shabby "Teddy" ever near,*
> *And when you hear her laughing to herself,*
> *Call all the Angels in – so they can hear."*

"Be good to her and give her all the things
That I can never give her anymore,
A puppy dog, a doll with golden curls,
A doll carriage and telephone that rings;
And Mary, when small Angels go to bed,
Lean down for me and kiss her golden head."

My mother and my father kissed Dorothy. "Don't you want to kiss your sister, too?" my mother asked. I bent over and kissed Dorothy on her lips. My mother said, "Oh! I meant you should kiss her on the cheek. You might get poisoned." I kissed Dorothy's cheek. Her cheek was hard and cold. The undertaker closed the lid of the casket.

We went outside. My father and mother sat in the back of the limousine. I sat on the little jump seat in front of them. I could see my classmates lined up behind the windows in my school room across the street. They had given a nickel each to send flowers for my sister.

We drove in procession to the Oak Grove Cemetery and past many tombstones until we came to a new section where a freshly dug grave gaped in the ground. We stood around the grave while the coffin was lowered. The minister crushed a rose over the casket as he said, "Ashes to ashes and dust to dust." The minister talked to my father and mother and then talked with me. He was the only one who seemed to know that I was grieving too.

The sun was still shining when we came home but the house was empty and cold.

When my mother felt ready to return to work, she was passing through a doorway on her way to the bathroom when the heavy door closure came loose and struck her on the head. When I came home from school that afternoon, I saw the lump on her head. She did not return to work for two weeks.

My mother and grandmother kept repeating that the head injury was a punishment for my mother's excess grieving over my sister's death. It was God's way of showing her that things could be much worse. As she was recovering from her head injury, I was sitting at her bedside. She grabbed my arm and said, "Oh God! If I should lose you too." I didn't much care about a God who had let my sister die.

When my sister died, I felt guilty because I resented the times my parents asked me to take her to dancing school. I had to walk a mile with her, wait at the dancing school until she was finished and then walk back with her. Although we were good friends and had a good time talking, as a 10 year old boy I found it embarrassing to be seen walking a girl to dancing school. Somebody must have teased me.

I decided that I would become a doctor and if I could save the life of one child, somehow the slate of my sister's death would be wiped clean. This is the way that my long journey began.

Mabelle Erickson with her two children, G. Walter, Jr. and Dorothy. Dothy's death at the age of 5 so affected G. Walter, Jr., that he made the decision to become a doctor and prevent the death of other children.

5. ILLNESSES

The only surgery I had as a child was a tonsillectomy. Most children during those years had their tonsils and adenoids removed whether they needed removal or not. My illnesses were usually respiratory. The standard treatment was chicken soup delivered by a sympathetic neighbor lady. If you had an ear ache, a washrag was warmed over an open hot air register and placed on the ear. Vick's VapoRub was applied generously to noses and chests and covered with a cloth. It was an uncomfortable worthless treatment but it gave the mother something to do. Years later I learned that the camphor in Vick's was dangerous. I could have told them that when I was a child.

Doctors rarely came to the house and children did not often visit the doctor's office. If a house call was necessary, the front walk was always cleared of snow and the entire house was cleaned. I was never hospitalized for an illness. The only immunization I received as a child was a vaccination against small pox.

Between 1860 and 1920 the serious diseases were typhoid fever, tuberculosis and pneumonia. In addition there were epidemics of diphtheria, scarlet fever and measles. There was little that could be done to treat these diseases. Hospital care was largely custodial.

Despite vaccination, smallpox was still around with a mortality rate of 24-30%.

6. SCHOOLS

ELEMENTARY SCHOOL

Our house at 382 Hancock Street was just across the street from Elias Brookings School. The school was built the same year that we moved into our house. The school building was surrounded by sidewalks so that most of the children became very good roller skaters. Ruth Elizabeth Playground was just behind the school. There was a football field, a baseball diamond, a soccer field, several basketball courts and a marble playing area. I almost forgot there were also 6 tennis courts where I spent most of my playtime from ages 12 to 16. Mr. Brittain was the all year superintendent. In the wintertime he flooded an area for an ice skating rink and erected a high platform for sledding. I still remember my violin teacher calling to me from the other side of the fence when I was playing baseball and should have been home for my lesson.

Although we had no car, it was only a short distance from our house to Six Corners where we could catch a streetcar. My neighborhood extended 4-6 blocks in all directions and further destinations were easily accessible by trolley. Three blocks away and just south of Six Corners, was the Asbury Methodist Evangelical Church for Sunday School, Epworth League and Boy Scout meetings.

The Ruth Elizabeth semi-pro baseball team was good enough to win almost every game. Each game had an overflow audience including every kid in the Six Corners area.

One of my childhood friends was Vic Raschi, later known as the "Springfield Rifle". He lived on Hickory Street on the southern border of the playground. When my mother had darned our family's socks to the utmost level, she gave me a bag of socks to take to the Raschi family. They were the only family we knew who were poorer than we were.

Vic pitched a no hit game for the Tech High School against Classical High in 1937. He played for area semi-pro teams until he joined the New York Yankees in 1947. He won 92 games and helped them win 5 World Series from 1949 through 1953.

Naylor and Bunny Tallifaro were two other ball playing friends of mine. Both were superb athletes. Bunny was the star pitcher of an

American Legion baseball team that was scheduled to play a team in South Carolina. When Bunny was threatened with bodily harm— because he was black—the whole team voted to come home.

In grade school we sat in circles and read. We took part in many plays usually historical in nature. In sixth grade I was elected to the Leaders' Squad. This was considered to be a great honor.

The Leaders' Squad had weekly meetings and received reports of violations of the School rules. If a student had three reports he was brought before the Leaders for chastisement. Thomas Crane had three violations, one of which was reported by me. When Thomas came before us I realized that his brother Ted was the culprit whose violation I had reported. I said, "I'm sorry. I made a mistake. His brother is the one I reported". There was a great silence and Tom Crane walked out a free man.

Once a week we went to a silent movie in the school gym. Joe Nickerson, one of my classmates, accompanied the action of the movies by playing the piano. The last I knew he was still playing at a local hotel.

The February after my sister died, we were graduated to Central Street Junior High School. I was 10 years old.

I had been a well-behaved student in grade school. At our graduation party I ruined that image. I decided to go as an Indian. Clothed in loincloth, blanket and armed with a kitchen knife, I made my entrance. My war whoops startled my classmates. When I threw aside my blanket and brandished my kitchen knife, I assured myself of first prize for the most unusual costume. No one disputed the award but I had ruined my image.

JUNIOR HIGH

The first year in Junior High, Miss Frances taught Social Science. Each week one row of students would give a report. Usually the report would be based on an article in the feature section of the Hearst Boston American. Each row was in deadly competition with the others. We would rapidly find the newspaper article, read it and be ready to question and criticize the presentation.

Miss Adams taught Nature. She did know her subject but she did not know how to handle male students.

Even though Miss Shapiro gave us a sampling of Latin, Spanish, German and French in the first year as a way to decide which language we wanted to study, we all chose French. It was the only foreign language the school offered.

Mr. Hannigan was our Shop teacher. He taught us practical tasks. I still remember how to install a doorbell.

Miss Price tried to teach Art. She had us draw a chair or a tree. She was very strict. One afternoon just before dismissal time, I said, "Miss Price. I feel sick. May I please leave?" "No," she snapped. "Wait for the others." My stomach couldn't hold out any longer and I vomited on her and her lovely Art Room. The students walked out without her permission.

For Gym, we walked to the playground to play softball, soccer or basketball according to the season. Since we were close to Springfield College, our instructor was usually one of their undergraduates.

We had our own print shop. We set the type and printed our 4 page Junior High Paper. At Christmas time we printed the paper in Red and Green.

In school, there was a girl no one seemed to like. She came from a poor Irish family and had a scar on her face from an old burn. One day at recess a large group of students began taunting her. She stood in the middle of the school yard surrounded by a group chanting, "Maggie O'Landy, Maggie O'Landy." I ran through the crowd to her side "If she's Maggie," I said, "then I'm her husband, Jiggs." The students laughed and shouted. They never expected such a comic ending to their taunting. After that they teased Maggie no more. (For those who don't know— Maggie and Jiggs was the most popular comic strip of the 1920s.)

In grammar school, relations with girls were simple. In Junior High girls became different and complicated. Doris and Eleanor were giggling in the back of the 7th grade room. Doris said to me, "You won't tell Miss Flaherty if I give you this note." I took the note and read it. The note contained a number of sentences that seemed to indicate that the girl liked me. I squirmed awkwardly because I didn't know what to say or do.

My two best friends were Richard Mayer and my cousin, John Waterhouse. We played tennis together almost every day in the summer.

7. ENTREPRENEUR

My first business experience was delivering newspapers. In my class there was an Italian boy named Augustino Delagusi. We called him Goosie. He owned a paper route near my cousin's home. Occasionally the newspaper trucks threw the bundles of newspapers closer to my cousin's house than to Augustino's. He asked me to help him deliver a few papers. Pretty soon I had my own regular customers. On Saturdays I received ten cents from Goosie and tips from some customers. I was impressed with the profitability of selling newspapers. Some nights Goosie wouldn't show up and I delivered the whole route.

Eventually, he wanted to sell and I wanted to buy. I was not quite twelve, which was the legal minimum age for a newspaper license, but my father took the route in his name. Thus, at ten cents a head, I became the sole proprietor of 29 customers.

Gradually, I increased the number of customers to thirty- five. My earnings averaged $1.50 a week. The price to the customer was 12 cents a week of which I paid 8 cents to the newspaper office and kept 4 cents as my profit. As well as I can calculate my rate of pay was 15 cents per hour.

Delivering newspapers on a regular route was fun. The other newspaper boys and I often had to wait 1-2 hours for the papers to be dropped off before we could start delivering them. It rained. It snowed and it was cold. But we solved that problem by playing football or roller skate hockey in the street or in the winter by having snowball fights.

After a year or delivering papers, I increased my route when another newsboy sold me his 90 customers. I paid 10 cents for each customer and $3 for his bike. The first few nights I delivered the 135 papers but I didn't finish until 7 PM and 8:30 on Saturdays. I had overextended myself. So I sold 10 customers to one boy and 25 to another and kept 90 customers who were located in a compact area. My $3 bike had long handlebars and a big basket on the front. Into the basket or on my back went all 90 papers. But first I had to fold each paper carefully, which allowed me to deliver my route in a little over one hour.

On Christmas Eve we received our newspapers free. Our customers were informed of this on Page One. I received many tips ranging from pennies to an occasional dollar bill. When I had completed my deliveries on Christmas Eve and hurried home to dinner and a tree waiting to be trimmed, I was the happiest boy on earth.

Life went on in the same way for two years. With my first $60 earned I bought an L. C. Smith Corona portable typewriter which I used thru high school, college, medical school and thereafter.

After a year of high school, I sold 25 more customers to my cousin. This left me with an even smaller but compact route that I could deliver in 35 minutes. By the time I left for college I had earned over $500 from peddling newspapers. In 1936 that would be equivalent to over $5000 today.

SISTERS

About a year after my sister's death, I noted that my mother was enlarging in her midsection. I finally realized that she was pregnant. Sure enough, I had a new sister on July 11, 1931. Her name was Norma Joan. She meant noise, diapers and bottles.

Instead of being an only child, I now was relieved from the pressure of my mother who was always worrying that something bad was going to happen to me.

In another 26 months, Marilyn Rose was born on September 23, 1933. By now I was an expert with babies. I knew how warm their bath water should be, how much weight they should gain and what their different cries meant.

I was twelve years old and in junior high school when Norma was born and 14 when Marilyn was born. My attention was not on my sisters.

By then I had found a girl friend. I was in love. By the time Norma was five and Marilyn was three, I went off to college so I did not know my sisters very well. The only time I came home from college was at Christmas. Also, I had some degree of feeling that no one could replace Dorothy.

COLLECTING STAMPS

Collecting stamps was a popular activity of the 1920-1930 era. We answered ads in the Open Road for Boys or The American Boy to "Send 5 cents in stamps or coin for sensational triangle stamp from Niagara and sheet of approvals". The stamp came, usually with a bunch of unused Germanics and sheets of approvals. I would spend a long time drooling over the approvals. Eventually I would select 10 cents worth of stamps and send the rest of the approvals back.

Saturday mornings we went downtown to Steiger's Store to meet Uncle Billy, an old stamp dealer. Afterwards we went to his shop and selected very carefully as much as a quarter's worth of stamps. Uncle Billy talked with us, totaled up our purchases and gave us bits of advice.

So strong was my interest in stamp collecting that it was responsible for my first serious disobedience. Ray Enos, one of my pals, was not only a stamp collector but so were his parents. We gazed in awe at their collections.

I was invited to a Stamp Party at the Enos house at 7:30 PM Friday night. Everyone who attended the party would be given a package of stamps. I wanted those stamps. "Can I go, Ma,? I asked. "No," she said. "It's too late." My father agreed with her. I had nowhere to turn.

At 7:25 on the night of the party I rode my trusty scooter to the party, stayed long enough to receive my stamp packet and scooted home. Cautiously I entered the kitchen door expecting a licking. My parents never said a word about my disobedience.

My homemade scooter was my mode of transportation. We took one roller skate and separated the front wheels from the back wheels. We attached the separate parts to a 3-foot board which was the base of the scooter. At the front of the board we attached an orange crate standing on its end. Across the top of the crate we placed another shorter board, which was our steering wheel.

This scooter served as my means of transportation from the time I gave up my tricycle to the time when I purchased my $3 bicycle when I was 12 years old.

I collected stamps all through Junior High School and High School. One day there was a notice in the newspaper. "William Sheldon, stamp dealer, died of heart failure in his home at 507 Bridge Street." To hundreds of boys he was known as "Uncle Billy." Without him to guide us in our stamp collecting, we might have strayed into other activities not so wholesome. As it was, he kept us occupied until Scouting came along.

8. BOY SCOUTS

Every Friday night the Boy Scouts met in the basement of Asbury First Methodist Episcopal Church. Came my eleventh birthday I began attending the meetings regularly. I could not become a Boy Scout until I was 12. My two best friends, Richard and John, older by one year could join and did.

Faithfully I studied the Scout Oath and Laws. I learned the history of Scouting and our flag. I learned to tie square knots and eight other knots.

Finally I was twelve and ready to be admitted. The scouts formed a circle of hands as I was led into the room. Inside the circle was the American Flag. The Scoutmaster asked, "Who is this candidate who seeks admission to our circle? Has he passed the required tests? Who will break the circle and admit him"?

John Plumb, leader of the Silver Fox Patrol, said, "We will." They broke hands, let me into the circle and with my hands grasping the flag, I began, "On my honor...." When I had finished reciting the Scout Oath, the Scoutmaster struck me on the shoulder and said, "I dub thee Tenderfoot Scout."

Standing in line with the other members of the Silver Fox Patrol, we repeated the Scout Benediction. "May the Great White Spirit of all White Spirits be with us until we meet again." As we finished, from a distance, a bugler played Taps. There was a moment of silence and the Scoutmaster said, "Good night, boys." A chorus of "Good nights" answered him and the meeting was over.

Scouting became a big part of my life from age 12 to 16. Carl Chauncey, a bachelor lawyer, was our Scoutmaster and devoted most of his spare time to our Troop. We hiked the White Mountains, the Green Mountains and every other hill in between. We took overnight trips to Camp Robinson in Westfield and 1-2 weeks stays in the summer at Camp Sherman in Brimfield.

Our Assistant Scoutmasters were Springfield College students. They were expert leaders of boys. Without the influence of scouting and Scout leaders, I wonder what would have become of me.

I had my first chance to be a radio star at the age of twelve. The Boy Scouts were presenting a 15-minute radio skit each Saturday at 2:15 PM. Our Scoutmaster wrote the scripts. He chose me to be Johnny, a Tenderfoot Scout, advancing through the ranks. We practiced after the Scout meeting on Friday night.

We met at WBZ the next day at noon and toured the studios and rehearsed in one studio, switching to the actual broadcast studio with a microphone. Then we did the real program.

As we finished each page, we dropped it softly on the floor. But since we did not fill up our 15 minutes of time, the announcer said, "There will be a brief musical interlude". With that two men played a piano behind us. One man played and the other man with a deadpan face slouched over the piano and plunked only two notes every few bars. We could hardly hold in our laughter until the program was over. Then we roared.

The following Saturday, we did another broadcast. This time we filled our time slot and felt like radio veterans.

The only lines I remember from the broadcasts are these: "There is a time to do the thing that's right—because it is right—as naturally as all things seek the light".

In February, a Mr. Donovan came to our school to organize a First Aid Club. About twenty of us joined and after several months of classes, we passed the exam to become Junior First Aiders. At the end of the classes, I asked Mr. Donovan why he was so interested in First Aid. He pulled out his left hand that he kept hidden in his jacket pocket, "Three years ago," he said, "I was in a bad auto accident. A well-meaning Boy Scout tied a tourniquet so tightly around my arm that by the time a doctor examined me, some of the nerves and blood vessels were damaged. Since then I've been trying to teach people not to make that mistake".

One day our Scoutmaster, Mr. Chauncey, said, "The minister has asked if Richard Mayer and you will deliver the sermon on Scout Sunday". We both agreed to do so.

Richard's theme was "Man is little lower than the Angels". I talked about the origins of the Scout movement and the development of its philosophy of helping other people.

One day in September, our entire Troop 33 marched down to the First Congregational Church (built in 1636) for a Court of Honor. I hoped I had made Eagle Scout. There was a moment of crisis when we reached the church. The Eagle Badge I was to be awarded had not arrived from Washington. My best friend went home and brought his badge for the ceremony.

After the other awards were given out, Walt Huffine stood up. "We have a very special award to present tonight," he began. I arose and stood before him. He laid his hand on my shoulder and continued. He talked for five minutes. I know. I watched the clock and I didn't hear a word he said. Finally he smiled, shook my hand and pinned the borrowed Eagle Badge on my chest. Everyone stood as I walked back to my seat.

In a scout meeting in September, the Scoutmaster announced that as the last Eagle Scout in our troop, I was appointed to escort a Governor around the Eastern States Exposition. The Exposition was held each year in the fall in West Springfield. Each New England state had a permanent Exhibit building and all the governors of the New England states were expected to come. An Eagle Scout was assigned to escort each governor. It was considered a great honor.

The day before the Exposition opened on Sunday the 17th of September, we met to receive our assignments. My assignment was Governor Cross of Connecticut. Accompanying us was a standard bearer and the route leader.

On Sunday, we arrived at 9:00 AM. Decorated with merit badge sashes, badges and clean uniforms, we waited an hour for the Governors to arrive. Each governor arrived one by one in a limousine with motorcycle escort.

Governor Curley of Massachusetts made a very impressive entrance as his limousine roared at 40 miles per hour into the Fair grounds. People scattered out of the way as the car came to a skillful racing stop. Gradually, the other governors arrived and were escorted away by the Eagle Scouts. Governor Cross arrived inconspicuously at about 11:20 AM. He greeted us cordially and then we took him on a tour. He posed for pictures in the Connecticut Building and proved to a gentleman. We escorted the Governors to a building where they had lunch.

We were free in the afternoon but we had to be back at 7:00 PM to escort the Governors into the Coliseum where each of the governors spoke.

G. Walter Erickson, in his Boy Scout uniform displaying the Eagle Scout award and 25 merit badges.

9. GRANDPARENTS

I was in my first year of High School when my grandmother died. One very early morning before I was up, I heard my mother running down the stairs outside my door. When I dressed and went downstairs, my mother was standing in her dressing gown. By listening to the conversation between my aunt and her, I gathered that my grandmother had started breakfast and collapsed on the floor. The doctor came. After examining my grandmother, he said, "There isn't much hope."

My mother became conscious of my presence and said, "Your grandmother is very sick. Whenever a doctor says that someone is seriously ill, that doesn't mean that the person will die".

However, grandma sank lower and died the next day. Arrangements were made for her funeral. Feeling sad I went over to my cousin's house. Needing something to do to relieve our feelings, we got out the boxing gloves and started to box. My great uncle, my grandmother's brother, reprimanded us, "Put those gloves away. It's disrespectful to be doing that when your grandmother is lying dead at home".

My grandfather never recovered from my grandmother's death. He refused to leave his room and ate all his meals there. His eyes grew weaker until he could not see at all. Two months later he had a stroke. There was no hope for an old man, lame and blind. Hour after hour he cursed my mother. He had never had an alcoholic drink in his life yet he yelled, "Bring me some wine." Sometimes quietly he called out, "Jennie, is that you?" (Jennie was his wife). Toward the last he repeated, "Jennie, I'm coming." He died peacefully in his sleep six months after his wife died.

It is an interesting fact that my sister, my grandmother and my grandfather all died at home. Being hospitalized was evidently not as common then as it is now. Was it the expense of the hospital? The fear of the hospital? The ignorance of the doctors as to the necessity of being admitted to the hospital? I don't know.

10. HIGH SCHOOL

My grade and junior high schools had been within a block of my home. High School was 2 miles away. Since the trolley car cost five cents each way, I walked to and from school. Actually I ran to school in the morning and walked home after school.

When the first marks came out, mine were disappointing. "Due, no doubt, " said a teacher, "to the fact that he received too much individual attention in junior high and is lost without it now." I knew better. My self-image was bad. Here I was in High School and still in short pants and singing in a clear soprano voice. Yes, I was a year younger and shorter than the others. I did not get a pair of long pants until I was fourteen years of age.

My first year in high school developed into a routine. I studied my Latin and German each night. Between 4-6 PM I delivered my newspaper route. Each Friday, I went to my Scout meeting and each Sunday to Church and Sunday School. Occasionally our Scout Troop went to Camp Robinson on weekends.

In the summer, most of our Scout Troop went to Camp Sherman in Brimfield for two weeks at a cost of $6.00 a week.

The following September when I started high school, Douglas Bray greeted me with wide eyes "Say," he said, "You've grown taller." Actually I had grown 5 inches. Now I could play basketball. We formed a team in the school league and did well. We played for the championship but lost by 2 points. We may have lost the game but I had won back my self-respect.

High school began again on September 7th. School, newspapers, church, Epworth League, Scout meetings came and went. When February came, the school moved all 130 seniors into Room 323. Spring passed quickly and on June 15th I turned 16 years old.

Again I went to Camp Sherman to earn my last Merit Badges to qualify for my Eagle Scout Award. For 4 years I worked through Second Class to First Class to Star to Life Awards. All I needed now was 10 more Badges for Eagle Scout

One-week at camp became two and then three. After two weeks, I had passed all but the Swimming and Life Saving badges. There were only five of us left out of 27 who had started the Life Saving classes. Our instructor was tough and unrelenting in making every phase of his classes very difficult.

Every night I said I would not go to class the next day. But the next morning I went. On the day of my exam for my Life Saving badge, I jumped in with all my clothes on, disrobed and swam 100 yards. I was able to do all the life saving carries but then I collapsed. That night at campfire, three names were read off as having passed Life Saving. My name was on the list.

Our Senior High School Banquet was held in February, 1936 in the Hotel Kimball's Party Room. After the food and the big wheel speeches, Helen Godfrey and Helen Gramse pulled out two chairs and pretended that they had just met in the future and began the Class Prophesy.

"Guess who I saw coming out of the Tribune offices yesterday! Walter Erickson—he's Editor and Publisher now, you know."

The other prophecies were in the same vein, all placing the individual at the top of some heap. Were it so that life could be so predictable.

Even though we were graduated from High School, it was the custom that February graduates continue in school until June and take postgraduate courses. I needed one semester of English. Almost all of the class planned to stay but the next morning the headline in the local paper read: "Schools to economize. Granrud (Superintendent of Schools) fears it necessary to cut out post graduate courses." There was controversy for days but he finally decreed that those who needed extra credit for college could stay.

We had review courses in Math, English and other subjects. At that time, Classical High School was recognized as the best high school in the United States. The teachers were outstanding. Our principal, William C. Hill, was world class. His philosophy, taken from Emmanuel Kant, stated "Don't do that which if everyone did would destroy society." He was always in contact with all the students and they respected him.

I continued to deliver my paper route each late afternoon, went to the movies on Saturday nights, to church on Sunday morning and to Epworth League Sunday night.

11. THE FLOOD OF 1936

Then on March 24th as we arrived at school at the usual time, we noticed that there were only a few people around. Principal Hill announced that the Connecticut River was overflowing and no school would be held that day. Longmeadow was cut off as were other lower sections of the city.

I hurried home, changed my clothes and went exploring. The riverfront was a mile over its banks. Water looked out of place on Main Street and was beginning to run through the side streets. Firemen in boots maneuvered quietly. Policemen stood at the edges of the water on sidewalks that were beginning to crumble. Only a few curious people wandered about.

By noon, families began leaving flooded houses. All afternoon the river rose and when I sat down to dinner, the radio was broadcasting one word: FLOOD. The announcer was sounding a warning, "All families within a mile of the river are advised to leave immediately. The waters have risen until they are within 10 feet of the record flood level of 1927. Thousands of families have been driven from their homes in Vermont and New Hampshire." His voice went on. "This broadcast is coming to you from Red Cross Headquarters on Maple Street where temporary broadcasting facilities have been set up to give you last minute reports of the flood."

I called Richard and John. "Let's go down to Maple street", I said. "They may need us".

My parents raised no objection. All my mother said was: "Be careful." I changed into my scout uniform.

When we reached the Red Cross building, we hardly recognized its changed appearance. A floodlight was directed upon its front. A steady stream of trucks, cars and motorcycles moved in and out. Police officers with lanterns snarled and unsnarled the traffic. Men in muddy boots and clothes walked in and out. Groups of men were standing here and there. Dr. Chapin and the Mayor were present. Over in the corner we saw a microphone.

A man was sitting at a desk in the center of the room. He was questioning people who stood in line before him. When we reached the head of the line, I said, "We're Eagle Scouts. Can we help?". "Yes", he said. "There's a truckload of food going out in a few minutes. See the driver over there" and he jerked his head to the left.

The driver said, "Hiya boys" and led us out to his truck. The truck was loaded with cases of food and cans of milk or water. "Wait here", he said, "I'll get armbands for you".

We stood in the back of the truck in the darkness. Now and then headlights would flash but sounds were muffled. We backed out and honked our way to the street. As we rode, we arranged the Red Cross armbands. We drove closer to the river until we came to an area that was full of noise. A chicken ran across the street in front of us. All the shop and house lights were on or so it seemed. Through the side streets we could see the waters reaching for us like long, icy fingers that kept drawing closer. Suddenly we stopped. We had reached a corner where a fire pump was fighting a losing battle trying to pump water out of the street. A man poled a rowboat back and forth. Ahead the water stretched in a continuous sheet.

Our driver talked with the men on duty. They shook their heads. The crowd watched curiously.

Our driver climbed back into the cab. We backed up a few feet and then slowly moved toward the water. We sank deeper until the water was over our headlights. The truck continued on at the same steady pace. On each side of us were empty houses. The ripples from the truck flowed out and washed on deserted steps.

After we traversed half a block, keeping careful watch as the water climbed up on the truck, we noticed that the level did not get deeper; in fact it began to subside. Ahead we saw dry streets and a policeman standing on a dry sidewalk. The water had surged around an entire quarter mile of high ground leaving it absolutely dry but isolated. We drove on across a broken street to a bridge. A squad of national guardsmen halted us with drawn bayonets. The driver explained his mission. The Squad leader held a lantern close to our armbands. "Proceed", he said.

We moved slowly across the now uneven surface of the bridge. Soldiers were stationed at various intervals. We lumbered across to ground on the other side and stopped in front of the Police Station. With the help of others we carried the food inside. Two officers were sleeping on cots in the outer room. Inside several other men sat around in various stages of dirt and undress. "Hello there, white boy," said one grimy policeman with a muddy face.

It was hot in the Police Station so we went outside. Sodium vapor lights blinked feebly beside the station entrance and at the entrance to a street. We took a tour of the area. At the head of each street was a line of rowboats and a man with a gun. "Why the guns?" we asked. "Looting" was the answer. "People left so quickly they didn't have time to take anything with them".

After a while we crowded into the truck and tried to sleep but in vain. We walked over to the bridge. The water spread in a continuous sheet across the land. As we walked onto the bridge itself, a patrol was changing guard. A line of muddy tired men stood on the road. In a few minutes, after a night in the mist, they were going inside for coffee, stale buns and a few hours of sleep.

We walked to the center of the bridge. The water swirled six feet below us, carrying with it trees, a chair, a table, pieces of houses. A whole house caught on one bank swung back and forth in the ebb. Over in the east, above the city, the sun began to rise. No factory whistles blew, no trolley cars rumbled along, no horns sounded, no people shouted. The only noises were the putt-putt of a motorboat, or the crunch of the sentry's boots behind us and the creak of oars and the swift rumble of water below. Gradually it became clearer. Nothing stirred. There was no movement except an almost undetectable sway of the bridge beneath us. It was morning— flood morning.

We drove back in about an hour. We were happy to crawl into bed. About 3 PM I arose to start prowling again. I went down to the waterfront and saw the boats of rescuers crowding the area. I wisely concluded that the best thing I could do was to stay away.

To make the situation worse, water seeped into the Electric Power Plant and shut off all city lights.

Our high school was turned into a dormitory for flood victims. Soldiers walked back and forth around the building. Inside many people ate, slept and lived. Nurses ministered by lantern light. Downstairs in the cafeteria, men slept on the floor, The principal's office was turned into a nursery. Women were quartered in the classrooms. Confusion and clutter were everywhere.

Homes were thrown open to flood victims and martial law was declared. Dr. Baumguard, a prominent neurosurgeon, attempted to enter the Armory to treat a patient and was refused entry by a National Guardsmen. When the doctor persisted, he was hit on the head with a rifle butt. This episode caused an uproar in an already tense community.

The floodwaters receded. Rehabilitation began. Water was pumped out of store basements. Flood sales were held. A new high-water mark was painted on the side of the Electric Light building.

The high school was the same except dirtier. The piano had initials carved on it and the whole school smelled of people and disinfectant.

Life went on.

CHOOSING A COLLEGE

On April 3rd, 1936 I sought advice from our school psychologist since I was undecided about my choice of college. After several hours of testing, we talked. We discussed Harvard, Yale and Antioch.

The idea of a cooperative college where I could alternate study and work might make college more affordable. For whatever strange combination of intelligent and absurd thinking, I applied for admission to Antioch College and was accepted.

But how was I going to pay for college? I had some money saved from my newspaper business. My parents had some savings but not enough. A school counselor suggested that the Horace Smith Fund might be able to help me.

Horace Smith had been a partner in the Smith and Wesson small arms company. He had much sadness in his life. His first wife died at age 31. An infant son also died. His second and third wives also died before he did. His son, Dexter, died at the age of 60, causing great grief to his father. Horace Smith died a few weeks later on January 15, 1893 at the age of 84 years.

THE FLOOD OF 1936 **41**

His will left money to several local organizations and to the Tuskegee Institute. The remainder of his money was used to create the Horace Smith Fund, the purpose of which was as follows:

"The aid of such educational, charitable and religious objects as may be worthy of aid and encouragement, and especially, but not exclusively and in imitation of the late Horace Smith, the aid of young persons in acquiring an education, either academic, commercial, industrial or professional."

The applicant had to be a resident of Hampden County. No limits were set regarding gender, race, creed or ethnicity. Four key questions were asked in regard to each applicant:

1. Has the applicant a genuine and firm ambition to fit him or her self for an occupation regarding more education than he or she now has?
2. Does he or she appear to have the ability to profit by the training he or she is asking the trustees to help him or her to get?
3. Is his or her financial situation and that of his or her family such that he or she cannot without undue hardship acquire the training without help from the Horace Smith Fund, but can do so with a reasonable amount of assistance from it?
4. Since the result of all sound training is to give more power to its possessor, is the applicant the sort of person who would presumably use this increased power in a way that would benefit any community in which he or she may live?

If in the opinion of the trustees the answer to all these questions is "Yes," the needed help is gladly given.

All payments were considered as loans that, although the obligation was moral rather than legal, were to be repaid without interest as soon as the beneficiary was able.

During the summer before I entered college and many times after, I found myself sitting in the cherry paneled study of Edward R. Appleton discussing my finances. Loans of $100 to $130 were made during the following four years. Without them I could not have gone to college.

Mr. Appleton was a trustee of the Fund and interviewed all applicants with dignity and interest in helping them plan their budgets. I remember him as a friend.

HIGH SCHOOL GRADUATION

The days of May faded into June. Came June 12th and high school graduation. Rehearsal was the day before where we greeted classmates whom we had not seen since February. Combined with the June graduates we totaled about 400.

After the Organ Prelude of Toccata, we marched into the Municipal Auditorium to the tune of the Coronation March from The Prophet. After everyone sang "America," Dr. James Gordon Gilkey gave the Invocation and the main address after the Glee Club and Orchestra played. After another orchestral selection, William C. Hill presented the classes for graduation and reminded us "Not to do that which if everyone did would destroy society."

Mayor Henry Martens shook hands with us as he gave us our diplomas and we marched out to face our brave new world.

12. NEWS REPORTER

Antioch College invited me as an incoming freshman to join a Thorne-Loomis tour of the western states. I accepted and looked forward to the trip. However, there were no spaces left and I had no other plans for the summer.

Previous to my consideration of the Antioch trip, I had applied for a position on the Camp Sherman staff but I had not heard from them.

I rode out to Camp Sherman with a family whose son was going to camp. I armed myself with a bunch of newspaper clippings about the Boys Club Camp. Their camp was also in Brimfield and there was a fierce rivalry between the two camps. Much information had appeared in the newspapers about the Boys Club Camp but nothing had appeared about Camp Sherman.

I found Walt Huffine, Camp Sherman Director, by the side of the Rec Hall. I showed him the clippings about the Boys Club Camp. "These," I explained, "have appeared in the Springfield papers since July 1st. There has been nothing about Camp Sherman". "By George, you're right", said Walt. He smiled. "What do you propose to do about it"?

"Write an article for the newspaper every day", I answered. "Let me take care of camp publicity".

Walt took a moment to decide: "All right, I'll let you try it. I'll let you have a week and we'll see how you make out".

By the time the parents were driving back to the city, I had a news article ready for the Springfield Morning Union. "Will you take my article with you and drop it in the nearest mailbox? I asked. "Better than that", they said. "We'll bring it to the Union office".

Monday morning I organized my routine. Walt gave me a typewriter and a desk in Doug Gladden's office. The lake was 50 yards away with the noises of swimmers, boats and canoes. The campers milled around the office, shouting and pushing.

It took three hours to write Monday's news story and it was only 300 words. I mailed it to the Union and waited for the mail to bring the newspaper to see if my Sunday story had been published. Eagerly, I unwrapped the paper, flipped page after page and there it was: "Camp

Sherman opens 2nd week". My article was 3 inches long. I cut it out of the paper and showed it to Walt. "Good", he said. "I expect to see one every day".

I set to work. I conferred with Clayton Moore and received the week's program in advance. I asked everyone to bring me any news they knew. I typed my articles oblivious of the disturbances around me.

At first, the other counselors were hostile but they enjoyed reading their names in the paper.

I realized after a few days that there were three newspapers in Springfield. I secured special News Envelopes for each paper and each morning I typed my dispatch for the Morning Union, changed it for the Evening Union, again for the Daily News and once more for the Republican. I included scores of baseball games, swimming meets and reported awards and special events. By 2:30 PM each day I had my copy ready for Brimfield and the 3 PM mail.

Then I turned to photos. I had a box Kodak camera. I snapped pictures, sent them in. Some were published. My finest moment came when the Sunday Republican printed a whole page of my photos and two were re-published by the Boston Post.

My world settled into a routine of 4 articles daily; photos whenever possible and specials for the Sunday papers. A camp election and a Fair helped provide material.

I contacted Felix, a news commentator on WSPR. He promised to use any material I sent him if it was limited to 500 words. I listened to hear if Felix used my material and how much he would change it.

He began," At Camp Sherman this weekend, they are having a gigantic Fair..." He went on reading my story word for word. What a thrill that was for me to listen to my words being broadcast.

I continued my publicity for the Camp Fair. On Friday I wrote my Sunday article "Fair at Camp Sherman attracts 500 visitors". Walt asked, "Aren't you putting that a little too high"?

Saturday night I looked over the Fair crowd in amazement. Booths had been erected all along the waterfront. Colored lights and sideshow tents created a true carnival atmosphere. By the time the Big Show started at 9 PM there were easily 500 people in attendance. "Shucks," I thought, "I should have said 1000".

CAMP COUNSELOR

The leader of the Bay Path unit for older Scouts was not doing a good job. Walt Huffine asked me to help him lead the unit. My life might have been peaceful except for the arrival of Dave, a young Jewish graduate of Harvard Law School. I met him one night in the deserted office as I was closing. "Visitor"? I asked. "No, I'm to be a counselor", he explained. "I've just finished Law School and I wanted some relaxation before I start work in the fall. I understand that Bay Path has been having some problems. What's the set-up"?

"Some of the leaders are not good, and some of the Junior Staff led by Clayton Moore are causing problems." We talked for two hours. Little did I know what would become of my peaceful existence.

An election by various units in the camp to select a Director and an Assistant Director for a day was scheduled in a few days.

At breakfast Monday morning, the Pearsall Unit announced their candidate for Camp Director: The Masked Marvel. He would be masked and his identity would not be revealed until after the election. The Smith Unit announced Pedro, a popular Italian boy as their candidate and other units announced their candidates.

Two nights later, at a primary election, the Masked Marvel and Pedro received the most votes. It was obvious that The Masked Marvel was way ahead in the voting. Although almost no one knew who the Masked Marvel was, everyone knew that Clayton Moore was behind him.

"Too bad", said Dave, "that we can't stir up a bit of opposition".

Next morning at breakfast, a spokesman for the Masked Marvel announced that at the election that evening the Masked Marvel would appear. Everyone cheered. It was apparent that the Masked Marvel would win in a landslide.

With the cheering still at its height, Dave stood up. "Just a minute," he began. "In Article XVI, Section 5 of the United States Constitution, it states that all candidates for office shall identify themselves. A candidate has to give his legal name. Therefore, I believe the candidacy of the Masked Marvel is unconstitutional."

There was a moment of silence and then almost all the Scouts were on their feet shouting. By voting time that night the camp was in an uproar and Pedro easily won the election. Dave had managed to change the sure election of the Masked Marvel into defeat.

Although Pedro had won the election, he did not appear at Reveille the next morning. We worried but Pedro finally appeared at 10 AM. He had been in hiding for his own safety. When he appeared, he quickly assumed control. He assigned the Masked Marvel to scrubbing pans and put Clayton Moore in charge of the garbage detail. A good time was had by all except for a certain few.

The most impressive part of the Camp day came each evening at Retreat. The members of the Junior Staff marched down the hill to take positions in front of the unit each one commanded. Then the Senior Staff members marched down the hill to stand in front of all the units.

After Walt Huffine had received the evening reports, "All present and accounted for, sir". He commanded "Attention". Then the flag was slowly lowered as the bugler played Retreat and a small cannon was shot off across the lake. At the sound of the shot, every staff member snapped to salute until the last bugle note died away. From there we went to Mess. On Sundays, with a full band playing and visitors watching from the hill, retreat could be very impressive.

After dinner I often took a canoe from the rack and paddled around the lake.

Finally came the last day of camp with the scouts leaving and the staff breaking camp.

By 4 o'clock most of the staff had left. Walt Huffine, the Camp Director, drove his car in circles around the field. "Hurrah," he yelled, "No more camp!" He was all smiles. "You did a great job on publicity. I hope you will come back next year".

Day by day I packed. I talked with Walter Ickgrath, a tennis player pal of mine. "Let me drive you to college", he offered. "How much will it cost you by train"? "Eighteen dollars," I answered. "All right", he said, "Pay me that and I'll take you right to the college door".

Sunday night all my relatives came over to say goodbye. Walt Ickrath came early in the next morning. We put my steamer trunk in the rumble seat of his roadster. I kissed my mother and two sisters, shook hands with my father and we were off. We stopped on South Main Street for gas and headed west on Route 20.

13. COLLEGE

Antioch was different than other colleges. I was to study and take classes for 10 weeks then work 10 weeks alternately all year long.

At the time, September, 1936, when I left Springfield, Massachusetts for Antioch College in Yellow Springs, Ohio, I had never been out of my home state except for some Boy Scout hikes on the mountains of Vermont and New Hampshire. My family had never owned a car and I had traveled very few miles in an automobile. Thus going off to college was a great adventure.

I remember no details of the journey. I only know that the travel on old Route 20 was uneventful. When Walter Ickgrath dropped my trunk and me off at the college, I had no further contact with him. Making a long distance phone call was not common in those days and men write few letters.

Two weeks of placement tests occupied full daytime hours. Evenings were consumed with roommate and hall mate adjustments. The rooms were just big enough to contain an upper and lower bunk bed and two small desks. The phone and bathrooms were at the end of the hall. There was, of course, no air conditioning.

The dining room was a block away on the first floor of the Women's Dorm. The Administration Building where most classes were held was a half-block away. A magnificent Science Building, given by Charles Kettering, was across the street. It was rumored to have cost the unheard of sum of $300,000. The Gym was nearby and a tearoom was two blocks away. These buildings plus a power plant and a Library were the major physical facilities of Antioch College for the 600 students.

My roommate was Bronson Clark who later became Secretary of the American Friends Service Committee. The other 20 residents of the hall were from many different states. All were in the top ten per cent of their high school classes and most were a year older than me.

FRESHMAN YEAR

As a Pre-Med major my classes consisted of Inorganic Chemistry, Biology and such. The Professors were very good in teaching their subjects. My science classes were in the new Science Building so the facilities were the best. I felt very comfortable that I had made the right choice of a college.

LIBRARY JANITOR

After 10 weeks of college as a student, I was assigned to my first job. Since I, at 17, was younger than the average freshman, the Personnel Department deemed it best that I not go off campus to a strange city. Accordingly, my first position was janitor in the College Library. My salary was $12 each week or 30 cents/hour which was double the hourly rate that I had earned as a paperboy.

Each morning I swept the library floors with a brush and broom. There was no vacuum cleaner. Theoretically I also dusted the books but not very often. I believe that my library could easily have won the competition for dirtiest library of the year.

In the afternoons I lettered the ends of books so that they could be seen more readily on the shelves. This part of the work was enjoyable as it gave me the opportunity to talk with and listen to the librarians.

I kept my job as library janitor during the work weeks my first year. The job allowed me to read books for my courses and otherwise. It was a good system for my first year of college.

When the first semester marks came out, I received a C-minus for almost every one of my courses. These marks disturbed me and I resolved to study harder and try to raise my marks to B and A.

When the second semester ended I awaited my grades with hope. In spite of dedication to studying, my grades had only improved from C- to C+. This was extremely discouraging to me and I began to wonder if I was capable of being a doctor.

SUMMER CAMP JOB

That summer Antioch offered me a job as Indian Counselor for the summer at Camp Knollsea at Lake Shelby in Michigan. It was a fun job with tepee building and arrow making and campfire meetings. The concluding event with all the parents present was an Awards Ceremony with the fire being ignited from the sky (via a wire strung from a tree).

14. COLLEGE – SECOND YEAR

I returned to college a little healthier and very confused. I decided to change from Pre-Med to Education since the Science courses seemed to be beyond my abilities. Accordingly, my choices were Accounting, Economics, Essay and Article Writing and Public Speaking.

HESSIAN HILLS JOB

At my 10 week break, the Antioch Personnel Department secured me a position at Hessian Hills School in Croton on Hudson, New York. This was a private school in a liberal community where Stuart Chase, Max Eastman and Floyd Dell now lived and where Edna St. Vincent Millay and Lincoln Steffens once lived.

I stayed in a boarding home with 10 students and assisted in a class at the school. In the evenings I often visited homes of faculty members to participate in discussions about world events. It was quite a change from conservative thinking in Massachusetts to the liberal almost Communistic colony of Croton on Hudson.

The school was one of the Associated Experimental Schools which included 59 Bank Street School in New York City begun when many professional, literary and artistic people moved to Croton on Hudson to isolate themselves from the evils of Manhattan but near enough to enjoy its advantages. Because of the poor quality of the village schools, the mothers began teaching their children. When the second year began, many families wanted to have their children join the group. In the 3rd year there were 29 pupils and the parents bought an old farmhouse to contain them.

The faculty increased to five and the name "Hessian Hills" was chosen because of the proximity of the hills where General George Washington fought the British Mercenaries.

By 1930 the school had increased to 78 children and 15 faculty. The parents who sent their children to Hessian Hills that year included Heywood Broun, journalist; Henry Carlton, playwright; Stuart Chase, economist; Floyd Dell, novelist; Dr. Adolph Elwyn, physician; Professor Austin Evans, Columbia University; William

Hodson, Director of Welfare, New York City; Henry Hunt, former Mayor of Cincinnati; Dr. Edward Liss, child psychiatrist; and Lincoln Steffens, author.

On the night of January 15, 1931, the Hessian Hills School burned to the ground with a complete destruction of all equipment.

In spite of this disaster and inadequate insurance, the school went on with the loss of only one day of class. Classes continued in a boarding house nearby. One parent gave $3000; another started a building fund; houses were thrown open; parents gave personal books.

The parents formed a non-profit corporation and raised enough money to rebuild a modern school designed by Howe and Lescaze of New York and Philadelphia.

When I was at Hessian Hills in 1938 there were three boarding homes, 88 students, 15 teachers, 10 classrooms, an auditorium, music room and a gym. I worked mainly in the classrooms with Alice Roth-child and Walter Clark, both of whom were master teachers. When I was not in the school, I lived in a boarding home with 10-12 children caring for them in sickness and in health.

I had my first experience in teaching children with specific reading disability. When I had total responsibility for a class, I found one student, usually a boy, who was disruptive." If only he were not in my class," I thought, "It would be easier to teach the others." I learned that I had to accept all the students and teach all of them. Teaching became fun and I thought that being a teacher might be my choice of a profession.

On my day off each week, I took the train from Croton on Hudson to Grand Central Station in Manhattan. I explored the entire island from Wall Street to the Village, from Times Square to Chinatown and Harlem. Usually I walked but eventually I learned to use the subway system. I went to Broadway plays and movies. I ate at the Automat and wherever dinnertime found me.

I studied New York City with the wonder of a New England adolescent who was not worldly wise. When my day off was over I caught the last train to Croton on Hudson and walked 3 miles to Hessian Hills School.

There was a small lake in front of the School. When the weather was warm we swam in the lake. When it was cold enough, we cleared off the snow and skated. One of my fondest memories of Hessian Hills was skating on the lake on winter nights under a full moon.

SUMMER VACATION JOBS

When school was over at the end of May, the mother of one of the students asked if I could stay with her children for the month of June. The $75 plus living expenses seemed huge compared to the $25 I had been receiving monthly at Hessian Hills. I gladly accepted her offer.

It was the best vacation I ever had. The family estate was in Croton on Hudson. With Betsy, Joan, Peter and Eva, I rode horseback, swam, rowed, played tennis, ate like a king and relaxed in the sun. The butler placed a glass of fresh orange juice at my bedside each morning. The horse trainer handled the horses. The chauffeur drove us into Manhattan in one of the 5 cars, the one with a glass partition between the front and rear compartments. Dinner was prepared by the chef and a maid served meals in the dining room.

Whenever there was an important dinner guest, I was invited to eat in the dining room with the guest and to participate in the discussion after dinner. I was treated like an honored guest by the nicest family I have ever met.

Two of the children in my charge were Peter and Eva Kugel who had just arrived from Holland. Because of the threat of the Nazi takeover, their family was forced to flee the country.

I received another offer to be a counselor at a camp at Sag Harbor, Long Island for July and August. The offer was made because Peter and Eva were to be campers there.

On July 1st we packed and drove to the camp. The site was a huge house, once a roadhouse, where 7 boys and 4 girls lived and we settled down with the mosquitoes and the heat. There were 2 other counselors and the Director. We used the house, the large fields and the beach for our activities.

I narrowed my career to education or medicine. The former seemed too easy; the latter, too difficult. Perhaps my attitude could be summed up by a remark a 15-year old boy flung at me," You haven't got the guts to be a doctor. All you'll ever be is a school teacher." I wanted to be a doctor but I was unsure of my ability for the first time in my life.

15. COLLEGE – THIRD YEAR

For my second year of college during which I had taken all non-science courses, I earned A or B in every one. In spite of the good marks and the enjoyment I had in teaching, I made another of my Great Decisions. I would return to Pre-Med for my third year in college.

I came back to college that fall with a grim purpose to get good marks in the technical studies of my first year. I winced when I registered for Analytical Chemistry, Physics Laboratory, Comparative Anatomy, Optics and Microscopy.

HESSIAN HILLS JOB AGAIN

At the end of 10 weeks, back I went to Hessian Hills for my second work year. I was given more responsibility at the boarding house and I taught more subjects at the school. Every Monday afternoon we had a meeting with Dr. Liss, a child psychiatrist or Charlotte Bridgeman, a child psychologist. Most of the terms and most of the references were over my head but I did store some factual residue.

In the classes I helped in at Hessian Hills, I was amazed to listen enraptured to the story the teachers unfolded. Frances Elwyn, who taught Biology, would bring a calf's heart or liver to class. I learned more American history than I did in high school. Then in the middle of the school year the children in all the grades met and decided to combine social studies into a Pageant of America. For 4 weeks, 90 children wrote, rehearsed, and made scenery for a project that combined singing, ballet, pantomime and acting to produce a great pageant.

The Pageant was hardly over when a full movie crew arrived to make a movie about our progressive education. Lee Dick, director of "The City" and his crew made the movie which was called "School". For 10 weeks I absorbed the making of that movie but unfortunately I have never seen it.

In January two refugee children came to the school from Vienna. Walter was 8 and Paul was 5 years old. Neither child could speak a word of English except "yes." I lived with them and tried to teach them English. I learned more German than they did English.

The cold weather of February seemed to be a signal for the children to become ill. Every child had chicken pox. The house was turned into a sick ward for one month. This was cause for further thought. As I watched Dr, King, the pediatrician, treat the sick, I observed how few drugs he pre- scribed and how much psychology he used.

Hans Zinsner wrote: *"The Doctor's profession is in part, an art—since it deals with matters which involve manual skill; in part, it is a branch of that vague middle ground between the physical and the psychological, in which emotional intelligence and great sanity of judgment are required."*

Despite the enjoyment of teaching and associating with children, I had the feeling of helplessness when they were sick. I also felt inadequate that I was trying to teach them how to live and I had limited experience in the real world.

NATIONAL BROADCASTING COMPANY (NBC) JOB

It was with this thought that for my next co-op assignment I sought a job at the National Broadcasting Company in New York City.

Another college student and I spent two days looking for a place to live in Manhattan. Every apartment we found was too large, too small or too expensive. At the last possible moment we were able to sublet Apartment 8E at 55 W. 11th Street in Greenwich Village

We reported to our jobs at Radio City. Measured for uniforms, we soon looked like any other page in white flannels, white shoes and socks, white dress shirt, black tie and dark blue coats with a microphone on one shoulder and GUEST RELATIONS STAFF on the other. To distinguish us as being on floor operations, we wore a blue lanyard on one shoulder.

At five each night we reported to line-up. There we were given our posts. At first we went to the eighth floor where we sat at a desk and answered the phones or stood at attention to say," Guests of Cities Service, this way please." On the eighth floor were Studios 8G and 8H from which the Vallee Hour, Town Hall Tonight, Cities Service, Firestone, Johnny Presents, Tommy Dorsey and Death Valley Days went on the air.

Seeing and talking with the stars of radio, Broadway and Hollywood cured any desire of being in their shoes. Those at the top could be as unhappy as those waiting for a break. The business of entertainment was a nerve-wracking exhausting job. When an entertainer came out of a studio after his or her performance, often the first person they saw was one of us Pages. Their first question was, "How did I do?" Even though we may not have seen or heard what they did, we always said, "You were great!" And they probably were.

After learning about the eighth floor, we were assigned to the third floor that had many smaller studios. RCA, Magic Key, Larry Clinton, Horace Heidt, Guy Lombardo, Hobby Lobby, Information Please, Manhattan Merry-Go-Round and a flock of sustaining programs were broadcast from there. Our duties on the third floor were the same as on the eighth floor but we had a more intimate contact with the performers. I'll never forget the night that Eleanor Roosevelt headed Hobby Lobby in Studio A with an overflow audience while across the hall in Studio B a trained seal was barking for George Jessel's Celebrity Program.

It was on the third floor in Studio 3H where all the live television shows were produced. One afternoon we were fortunate enough to crowd into the control room of 3H to watch a rehearsal. Three members of the cast sat in a living room set. Three cameras were in various positions, each operated by a tropical-helmeted engineer and maneuvered by an assistant. Another man controlled the boom microphone. Twenty banks of 12 spots each beat down on the players who wore sunglasses during rehearsals. The actors talked and moved in the living room as one camera took a long shot, another moved in for a close-up and a third came in from a different angle. Every minute or less, the director, seated in the control room and watching each of the pictures being taken by the three cameras, would cry "Stop!". Camera angles, lights, position of the actors had to be perfect because in these beginning days of television no re-takes were possible. That is why each hour on the tube needed twenty hours of rehearsal.

Some nights we went down to the Main Hall to control the crowds coming into the elevators to take them to be the Studio audiences. Main Hall, also known as Purgatory, had air conditioning but the large number of people made it as hot as Hades. We stood at the ropes and checked each person who came through. We became very skilled in controlling crowds of people but we made mistakes. An old NBC story tells of a night when there was a big charity program. Of the thousands who filed past him, the page on duty challenged two people, Mayor LaGuardia and Lily Pons.

The prize assignment was in "Programs". This meant that we checked tickets at the Studio Door and stood inside the Studio before and during the program.

It was exciting to be in the Studio during the actual live broadcast but it was boring to hear every master of ceremonies greet every studio audience in the same way.

"Good evening, ladies and gentlemen," he'd say. "I want to welcome you to the Vallee Hour. We know you're tired, had a hard day— maybe been out to the Fair. We want you to just relax and enjoy yourself. Loosen your collar, take off your shoes if you like. There's one thing, though, that I would like to ask of you. You know, we of the theatre live by applause. Money is the last thing we think about— before going to bed at night. When I raise my hands like this, applaud as loud as you can and maybe Aunt Minnie out in Iowa will hear you. Let's try it once. (APPLAUSE) That's fine, but there is a lady in the third row who has gloves on. Let's try it again. (MUCH LOUDER APPLAUSE) Well, I do declare, I think this is the best studio audience we've ever had."

"Thirty seconds, Mr. Kent," says the engineer. The lights dim, the announcer skips to his panel, the orchestra leader raises his baton, the cast gathers around their microphones and the sound man poses at his turntables. The second hand glides to twenty seconds before the hour. The NBC chimes are rung. "This is WEAF New York," says the announcer. As the second hand reaches zero, the director inside the control booth points his finger at the M.C. and the program is on the air.

In addition to our regular assignments, we all went to class. For two weeks we studied the National Broadcasting Company and spent another ten days in television training. We were then ready to conduct Studio and Television Tours. (Price: fifty-five cents each or ninety cents if both tickets were bought at the same time.)

Wearing white lanyards to denote Studio Tour, we met our group of 30-40 tourists on the mezzanine. After suitable introductions, we took them to the fourth floor. We checked with the Page's desk to note which studios were available. We explained to the tour what they were about to see and hear. Then we led them into an observation room overlooking the studio. The guests could hear the announcer or actors in the studio thru a loudspeaker in the booth. Each studio was suspended from the building to isolate it from all outside vibration and noise.

The guide did not talk much while in the booth. We identified the persons in the studio. We pointed out the announcer, engineer, program director, sound effect and set-up men. We also indicated which programs originated from each particular studio.

We visited as many studios that were active on the 4th floor. The tourists asked questions freely because we could not be heard in the studios. We pointed out the Client's booth which was a small observation room where the sponsor and his guests could observe and listen to the program.

As the grand finale we took the group inside an actual studio where we, the pages, had the opportunity to be the star. We demonstrated how sound effects were made. We did animal sounds, horses galloping, doors opening and closing, thunder, wind and rain. As the instruction manual states, "A sense of showmanship is necessary to sell this exhibit."

Since many of the pages were show business hopefuls, they took advantage of this opportunity and put on great productions.

We also went into the observation room which overlooks Studio 8H, the largest broadcasting studio in the world at that time. The room was two stories high and seats 1400. It "floats" like the smaller studios. Toscanini, The Fitch Band Wagon and the Fred Allen Show broadcast from this studio.

By the time the Radio Tour was over, most guests had enjoyed the tour and were suitably impressed. Each of them had some facts and stories to relate to their relatives and friends back in Ohio or Montana or elsewhere.

Television was developing enough to have a tour of its own in 1938. We did not have much to show but what we had was exciting. Decorated with our red shoulder lanyards to indicate our TV Tour Guide status, we started the tour by explaining the photo-cell in the elevator. NBC and RCA had been experimenting with television for 10 years. Two years later the work was moved into the Radio City studios and a series of experimental programs were broadcast from the transmitter on top of the Empire State Building. The broadcasts were received by NBC executives on experimental receivers located in various areas of Manhattan.

This is what we told our guests on the TV Tour. We explained that the development of the photo-cell which changes light into electricity was the key to understanding the miracle of television. Zworykin and other RCA engineers developed a new method, using two glass tubes to make the pictures electrically and eliminate bulky mechanical equipment.

We didn't understand much of what we were telling our guests. We said to remember the words "iconoscope" and "kinescope" but none of us did.

What we did on the Tour made it all worthwhile. We interviewed each guest on TV camera in one room which the members of the Tour watched in another room. This was thrilling to all of us and the guests really had something to tell the folks back home.

The Studio and Television Tours were timed to last forty-five and thirty-five minutes respectively. On nights when we were busy and tours were leaving the mezzanine every five minutes, it was essential that every phase of each tour go off on schedule. With 90,000 people taking the tours each month, the mezzanine was overflowing all day from 9 AM to 9 PM.

My best assignment was yet to come. On the second floor was a 70 foot long desk. Whoever sat behind this desk greeted many guests, actors, actresses, singers, musicians, i. e., anyone who worked or entertained at the National Broadcasting Company. It was a fun job.

What made the position even more interesting was a peculiar characteristic of radio broadcasting in those days. Many of the more popular programs, which were broadcast in the early evening, were repeated live for the west coast stations later at night. I had control of the tickets for the late night live broadcasts and I knew how many tickets were available. I would call my friends and have them use the tickets. There was nothing illegal or underhanded about what I was doing but I did develop a lot of friends.

The Fred Allen Show was a good example. The original live broadcast from Studio 8H was on at 7 PM. Fred and Portland rebroadcast live at 11 PM. The early show was always full but there were plenty of tickets for the late show.

The second floor desk was elevated and had a good view of the opening elevator doors. Through those doors walked many of the important and interesting people of broadcasting. Sooner or later just about everyone appeared. The game I played was "Guess who I saw last night."

I saw and heard many of the popular bands: Larry Clinton, Guy Lombardo, Glenn Miller, Tommy and Jimmy Dorsey and Fred Waring.

One Sunday night I delivered a telegram to Glenn Miller on stage in 8H just before a Fitch Band Wagon program. Even though he was involved in many details just before the broadcast, he was calm and kind.

Another memorable moment came on a late Saturday afternoon. I was on duty alone on the 8th floor when Milton Berle came in. He had to prepare a 30-minute program for broadcast later that night which he had not yet prepared. He asked me to help him. I observed this genius put together a great program from scratch. It was my most interesting hour at NBC and I became his admirer for life.

Television programs were just beginning when I was at NBC. From my post on the 3rd floor, I would sneak into Studio 3H and watch the magical mechanics of television. From the control booth I could see the three jeeps (cameras) dolly for shots and the boom microphone noiselessly following the action. Bill Eddy and Eddie Albert were the guiding geniuses of television and it was easy to be caught up in their enthusiasm.

Since my work at NBC was from 5 PM until midnight, the daytime hours were available to explore the museums and neighborhoods of Manhattan. On slow nights at NBC I might be off work at 11 PM leaving time to explore Greenwich Village after dark. Beer cost 10 cents a glass and I could safely roam the streets of the Village until the wee small hours. There were many small nightclubs with good jazz players. You could stand at the bar for hours for the cost of 1 or 2 beers

Even with my $15 a week salary, I managed a full life. Only one time did my finances almost fail me. I was due at work at 5 PM one night and all I had was 25 cents and a subway token. I went to the Life Cafeteria where, for 25 cents, I had a bowl of vegetable soup with all the crackers I could eat. I used my subway token to get to work where I collected my $15 to sustain me for another week.

The only problem with New York City was the heat. It was summertime and the living, except at NBC, was hot.

16. COLLEGE – FOURTH AND FIFTH YEARS

In September I returned to college for my 4th year. I continued with my pre-med course and scheduled Organic Chemistry, Embryology, Psychology and Government. Before I could began serious studying I found myself in Stag Hall as one of the older members. Now, because of the training I had received at Hessian Hill School and NBC, I could not be in any group without assuming command. The result was I was elected Hall President.

It was difficult at first. You can't treat your contemporaries as 12 year olds or as a Tour Group. I did know how to motivate people and get things done. Organizing the first Div Dance of the year precipitated me into the social whirl. I never knew before how much planning there was to hall parties, meetings, athletic teams and other details of hall functions.

Stag Hall which had been a dud in athletics and social life the year before, came back to win the basketball and football championships of the school and initiate a social program that made its name perhaps even too well known. We held Faculty- student meetings at which a faculty member came to the hall and talked with the students.

My study habits suffered as a result of my Hall activities but I did receive A's in Embryology and Psychology.

Several weeks after the final Psychology exam, I was walking across campus, Professor Leuba stopped and asked me a question. "Did you cheat on the final exam?"

All exams were given on the Honor System so that there was an opportunity to cheat. "No," I answered. "Why do you ask me?"

His answer was: "You are the only person ever to score 100% on the final exam."

There were several reasons why I had done well. First I loved the subject and had read every psychology book in the Science Library. My favorite book was one titled "Straight and Crooked Thinking." The book did not mean honest and dishonest thinking. It meant thinking in a straight line instead of a curved or confused way." Why are we here? What is our objective? What is the direct path to get there?"

That one book was the most significant book that I read in college. It helped me pass the Psychology exam and it has guided my thinking all my life. I shall try to give you an example.

There was an important conference regarding Cesarean Sections at Memorial Hospital. The number of Cesarean Sections was rising at the hospital and evidently the Joint Commission on Hospitals and the Hospital Administration were concerned. The discussion went around in circles for one hour. Then I asked a question which should have been asked at the beginning.

"Has any doctor ever been sued for doing a Cesarean Section?" The answer is "very rarely." In the presence of maternal or fetal distress, a doctor may be sued if he does not do a Section. Therefore in our present litigious society, there is no realistic way to reduce the incidence of Cesarean Sections.

NBC AGAIN

At the next 10-week work period, I went back to NBC. This time I lived at 96 Perry Street in Greenwich Village with 3 other Antioch students who had various jobs in Manhattan. Rent was $60 a month (divided 4 ways). Another $30 each a month covered telephone, gas, laundry, electricity and food. In other words, $45 each took care of all of our living expenses per month. The only other expense was an occasional growler of beer at 25 cents per man. (A growler is a 2-quart bucket which you take to the nearest tavern to be filled with beer and consumed at home.)

As Christmas was approaching and I was free during the day and needed money to buy presents, I applied at Macy's Department store for a Christmas job. I sold electric trains at Macy's from 9 AM to 5 PM and worked at NBC from 5 PM until midnight.

Back at college again after Christmas I continued with my Science courses.

SELLING LINCOLN LIBRARIES

I wanted to work in a hospital for my next work period but no positions were open. The Personnel Department sent four of us to the Frontier Press in Columbus, Ohio for a week's training. Frontier Press was the publisher of the Lincoln Library, a one-volume encyclopedia.

I was assigned to the town of Lancaster, 30 miles southeast of Columbus. Our purpose was to go door-to-door to the homes which had children of school age and try to sell their mothers the Lincoln Library for $16.50. I sold nothing for the first 10 days but over the following 4 weeks I managed to sell 16 books.

I remember walking along Lancaster streets in April looking in the windows and listening to the radios blaring, "Call for Philip Morris!" It reminded me of the days when I had been in the studio at NBC with that program and it made me realize the effectiveness of radio advertising. The radio had access to the home and was giving its complete sales pitch. I was competing on the outside trying to give the customer my sales pitch too.

Mr. Seibert, the sales manager of Frontier Press came to Lancaster to demonstrate how to sell. As pure as if he had stepped from the pages of Thornton Wilder's "Heaven's My Destination," he could sell books to women. I never reached his competence but I did become more confident in approaching customers and I did learn to be persistent. The 5 weeks of door-to-door selling were the most frustrating time of my job experiences but I did learn how to sell.

SUMMER AT LAKE OF THE WOODS, CANADA

Summer came and with it an opportunity to vacation on the shore of Lake of the Woods in Ontario, Canada. Nate Gilbert invited two other classmates and me to spend 1-2 months near their family cabin. We drove to the Lake and went by motorboat to the cabin area.

We lived in two tents in the woods. For milk we had a goat. For food we had a lake full of wall-eyed pike. We made our bread and ate our fish baked, stuffed or smoked. It took only a few minutes to catch a fish when we dropped our line into the lake.

Our favorite sandwich was peanut butter and slices of raw onion on our freshly baked bread. The moist onion balanced the dry peanut butter.

Summer was uneventful except for a few episodes. A black bear crashed into our tent one morning. Deer were visible in the woods but none of us had any desire to shoot them.

On one afternoon we decided to visit Sioux Narrows, an Indian and fishing community at the northern end of the lake. We went by boat (which was the only way we could travel) and had no difficulty in getting there. Returning home was a different matter. Lake of the Woods had hundreds of small islands and they all looked the same. It did not help that we were returning at night which was pitch black, raining and cold.

We ran the boat motor at a very slow speed with a lookout peering over the bow. Without warning we bumped into the sandy shore of one of the islands. We decided that the safest course was to stay overnight. The problem was that it was cold and raining and we had only one dry match. We gathered wood and somehow managed to start a fire which kept us warm until daybreak. We motored back to our camp in the daylight.

FIFTH YEAR

At the beginning of summer I had twenty dollars. At the end of summer I had ten dollars. Although I had earned no money, I had acquired a great reserve of health which could carry me through the next tough years.

On the way back to civilization, I stopped to talk with Gerhard Hartman, Secretary of the American Hospital Association and Director of the Hospital Administration Course at the University of Chicago. I had been thinking of Hospital Administration as a possible career. His advice to me was to go to medical school and then consider Hospital Administration.

My conclusions were that I would continue my pre-medicine journey, apply to medical schools and concentrate on raising money for medical school.

I rode a bus to the edge of Chicago. Then I used my usual mode of transportation to get back to college: I hitchhiked. In Hammond, Indiana it took 5 minutes to get my first ride to Kokomo with a punch-press operator. After a 40-minute wait I had a ride with a real estate man to Indianapolis. I took a trolley to Highway 40 and had a ride with a factory worker to Dunreith. It took 20 minutes to get a ride with a ship-builder to Springfield; 5 minutes to get a ride with a black divinity student to Yellow Springs. Total cost of transportation for my journey was 44 cents plus 36 cents for breakfast and 30 cents for lunch.

Under the co-op plan of alternate work and study, it took 5 years to obtain a college degree. Thus, I was returning to Antioch for my 5th year. My subjects were Organic Chemistry, History of Ideas, Survey of Western Literature, Courtship, Marriage and the Family.

I was also a Freshman Hall Adviser so I returned early for Freshman Week. Because of my NBC training and experience, I enjoyed the details of Freshman Orientation.

BUDD MANUFACTURING COMPANY JOB

In October I went away on a co-op job again. This time, with medical school in mind, I had one purpose: to earn money.

Reporting to the Budd Mfg. Company in Philadelphia, I began insulating railroad cars. I sprayed a black liquid inside the cars and then installed fiberglass insulation. It was a dirty job with black goop and fiberglass all over me and my clothing. My shoes were so filthy that I had to wear my Indian moccasins to a dinner at a private home.

After one month at the RR cars, I welded truck seats on a piece meal basis. This meant that the faster I worked, the more money I made.

When I returned for a subsequent 10 week work period, I was assigned as janitor at another area of the Budd factory. I began my college career as a janitor and now I was ending the same way- as a janitor. The difference was that my salary had increased from twelve dollars to $35.00 a week.

After one week of sweeping the factory, I was promoted to assisting a welder but in one week I became the welder. We used copper arc welding. I usually was welding 12 feet in diameter smokestacks for ships. Large arms of the welding machine were held by a hoist and I made the two arms come together to make the weld on each side of the pieces. My boss did not think I was a very good welder but when I left to go back to college I became essential.

Factory work could be difficult but the pay was good. The second shift, 3PM to 11 PM, was the best. Sometimes I had to work the third shift, 11PM to 7AM and that was the worst. If you worked the second shift, you could get a good breakfast at the restaurants near the factory for 25 cents. Breakfast included grits, scrapple, bacon, eggs, and toast. It was at this time that I began my one dollar a day food plan: 25 cents for breakfast, 25 cents for lunch and 50 cents for dinner.

I came away from working at the factory with an added appreciation for the joys of living and the beauty of the world without noise and swearing and missing fingers. I know what it is to be a factory worker and I have great admiration for them

EVALUATION OF MY COLLEGE EXPERIENCE

I arrived back on campus in January to begin my final semester of college. As a pre-med major, my subjects included most of the science courses. Except for my second year detour into education and business, my schedule had been on target to complete all the required subjects for entrance into medical school.

My most important final college project was to complete my senior paper which was an analysis of courses, teachers, jobs and complete Antioch experience. Would four years at a normal college have been better for me? Who knows?

Antioch gave me various experiences in many places and positions which I would not have had at an ordinary college. From Yellow Springs, Ohio, to Shelby, Michigan; Croton on the Hudson, New York; New York City, Sag Harbor, Long Island; Lancaster, Ohio; Lake of the Woods, Ontario, Canada; Philadelphia, Pennsylvania. From janitor to Indian Counselor, teacher, Page and Tour Guide, Camp Counselor, door to door salesman, to janitor factory worker, and welder. I took the road less traveled and I had fun along the way.

Dr. Morse, obstetrician-in-chief of the New Haven Hospital said, "It seems to me that your experiences have been the best possible kind for a doctor. You have learned how to deal with people of all classes when they are well and you will find that you will be better able to heal them when they are sick".

Every teacher and every job helped me in my development..
In conclusion I quote from my Senior Paper

"On the front campus of Antioch College is a statue of Horace Mann, the founder of the college. At the base of the statue is an inscription: *BE ASHAMED TO DIE UNTIL YOU HAVE WON A VICTORY FOR HUMANITY.*"

"I know that the solution in the world's ills lies not in sentimental impulse but in an attack on fundamental causes and the attack can be made in a hundred different ways. The teacher, the engineer, the business man, the social worker, all are important in making the world a better place. I have chosen my approach. It is no more direct or valid that that of any other but to me it is real."

"Next September, I enter Medical School. I have already received my acceptance. To say that I look forward to it is an understatement. It represents the culmination of my entire philosophy of life. Hans Zinsser wrote: *"Medical training embraces a broad survey of the biological field, enforces a considered correlation of the fundamental sciences and on the human side brings the thoughtful student face to face with the emotional struggles, the misery, the courage and cowardice of his fellow creatures – to say nothing of the familiarity it gives him with sociological conditions, vice, crime and poverty. It is a balanced education of the mind and spirit, which in those strong enough to take it, hardens the intellect and deepens the sympathy for human suffering and misfortune."*

"Some day to every man there comes that time when stripped by fear of death of the tinseled harlequinade of worldly things, he lies there wondering and afraid. When that time comes to me, I want to be able to say, the victory I won for humanity was – not to have discovered some great new medicine, but to have saved the life of one child."

SUMMER HOTEL JOB

I left Yellow Springs, Ohio on June 10, 1941 after 5 years of college. I had no graduation ceremony. I had no training or skills that enabled me to earn a living.

My major in college was Pre-Med. I would receive my AB degree if I completed my first year of medical school. I had only one factor working for me. I had been accepted in medical school.

Along with some of my college mates, I rode a chartered bus to Springfield, Ohio where we boarded a New York Central RR train for the ride home. As we were all seasoned travelers, being veterans of a cooperative college program where we changed college and work every 10 weeks, we quickly dismantled the coach seats to provide sleeping quarters.

After an all night ride we reached Albany, New York at 6 AM just at sunrise. I had to change trains at Albany as the main train was continuing on to New York City. Ordinarily, I would have welcomed the chance to get off the train and have breakfast but I had no money.

When I arrived in Springfield, Massachusetts at 9 AM there was no brass band to greet me. My parents were at work and my sisters were at school. I had no luggage. All my possessions from 5 years of college were in a steamer trunk that would arrive in a few days.

So there I was, 21 years of age, 3 months from entering medical school and back in the same room in the same house that I had left 5 years before.

I was home for the summer for two reasons. First, I felt I owed it to my parents and my sisters because I had not been home very much for the past 5 years. Second, I needed to earn money for medical school expenses and living at home would reduce my overhead. The problem was finding a job. There were very few openings for a pre-med-student with no marketable skills who was available for only 3 months.

The position I found was as a bellboy at the Hotel Kimball in my home town. The hours were 6 PM to 6 AM, 7 days a week. The salary was zero. My income would come from tips only. I also had to hose off the front walk and steps before I went home in the morning.

My usual tip was a quarter for carrying bags to a room. If I brought a bottle of liquor to a guest, I might earn one or two dollars. We had a revolving door at the one of the hotel entrances. Late one night two drunks arrived in a taxi. One of them gave me $5.00 to take his companion to his room. The two men came through the revolving door and followed it around and out to the taxi where they drove away. Alcoholics were a big help to my income.

My income totaled $35.00 each week for a grand total of $400.00 for the summer. Compared to the $15.00 that I had earned at NBC in Manhattan where my living expenses were much higher, it was a good income.

My daily schedule became routine. After work at 6 AM I walked home, ate breakfast and slept until 4 PM when I again ate and then walked to work. My only expense was $5.00 to join the YMCA for the summer so that I could swim before work on some afternoons.

The summer ended and with a suitcase full of clothes and my typewriter, I was off to medical school. I rode south on the New York, New Haven and Hartford train to New York City. I visited familiar places in Manhattan for two days and then embarked on a train to a strange world where I had never been, Richmond, Virginia.

17. MEDICAL SCHOOL

FRESHMAN YEAR

I don't remember where I slept the first few nights in Richmond but I soon took up residence at the Theta Kappa Psi House at 1105 East Clay Street.

My room was on the third floor in the back with an adjacent bathroom with a tub—no shower. The disadvantage was that students in the other two rooms on the floor had to go through our room to the bathroom. But the advantages of living at this house were many. The house was directly across the street from the Dental School where my classes and labs in Anatomy, Histology, Pharmacology and Physiology were held. Rent was only $10.00 a month. By limiting my food budget to one dollar a day I could get by. My roommate was Harry Stoeckle, a fellow classmate from Antioch College.

After purchasing a stethoscope, otoscope, ophthalmoscope, percussion hammer, sphygmomanometer and microscope, I really felt that I was on the road to becoming a doctor.

After adjusting to hominy and grits, I settled into what would be my routine for the next straight 36 months. Because the year was 1941 and my country was at war, summer vacations were cancelled. I had a schedule that accounted for every hour in the day from 6 AM to midnight. If I were to flunk out, it would not be from lack of trying to study every available minute. Saturday night from 6-10 PM was the only free time. There was some alcohol consumption but only on Saturday nights. We were too scared. We had been warned that our social conduct was being watched to be sure that we met the moral requirements for becoming physicians.

Anatomy was my big concern because I had been told by a psychologist who tested me that I lacked structural visualization and therefore might flunk anatomy. In the Anatomy lab we were to dissect cadavers. Ours were shriveled old bodies immersed in formaldehyde between dissections. My lab partner was a brilliant scholar from Brooklyn but he would not touch our cadaver. Instead he read the directions while I did the dissection. Dr. Osterud, an intense Norwegian, was the Professor of Anatomy. Half way through my freshman year, he called me to his office. "Some of your classmates think you are working too hard. I want you to know that medical school is a long journey." This was the message from a perfectionist who usually told us that we were not working hard enough. My hard work paid off. I received "Honors" as my Anatomy grade. I give great credit to the psychologist who told me that I might flunk Anatomy.

One day, during Anatomy lab, we saw the bodies of two young men, who had just been electrocuted for some crime, being brought in for use in the next class. This spectacle turned me for ever against capital punishment.

Pharmacology was a major course taught by Harvey Haag. In 1941 there were no antibiotics. Sufanilamide had just been introduced in Germany but had not crossed the Atlantic Ocean. We were probably the last medical school class to learn the basics of Pharmacology because simple pharmaceuticals were the only ones available at that time. Somewhere along the way the art of prescription writing has been lost. Ask any pharmacist.

Pharmacology class was serious but we did have an annual "Harvey Haag Day". We came to class in the morning in our pajamas and presented Dr. Haag with a bottle of Haag and Haag Scotch. Dr. Haag often smoked a cigar in class and laid the cigar on the desk when he turned away to the blackboard. A student would seize the cigar and start smoking it. On Harvey Haag Day, Dr. Haag quickly turned back toward the student with hammer and nail and secured the cigar to the desk. This is probably not funny to others but I still remember Harvey Haag Day 50 years later with a smile. He taught with precision and with humor. He obviously enjoyed teaching and we enjoyed him.

Physiology was a dreaded class. There was so much to learn and we were so ignorant. The textbook was thick and the lab work overwhelming. We must have performed muscle-nerve studies on all the frogs in Virginia.

To learn the principles of anesthesia, we used ether and then chloroform on a dog. With ether the respirations stop with an overdose before the heart stops. With chloroform the heart stops before the respirations with an overdose. This is why chloroform is not used in the

United States. But several years later at New York City Hospital, I was giving drip ether to a child when he became restless. The supervising Anesthesiologist took a small vial from his breast pocket and administered a few drops to the child who immediately quieted down. What was in the vial? Chloroform!

Physiology also taught me how important motivation can be. In studying digestion it was necessary that some one of our group of eight students swallow a stomach tube to collect gastric juice. Each of the other members of my group tried and failed. It was my turn. I am so squeamish that I won't let a doctor use a tongue blade to look at my throat. But being determined to become a doctor, I swallowed the tube and collected the gastric juice.

One of the most dramatic first encounters with disease were the long lines of patients at the Syphilis Clinic. These patients received weekly injections of Mercury and Bismuth, one intravenously and one intramuscularly. The treatment extended over a one or two year period. We saw many patients with primary, secondary and tertiary syphilis. We soon learned the phrase "one night with Venus is not worth one year with Mercury".

The specialty of Dermatology was known as "Dermatology and Syphilology". By far the greatest part of Dermatology was the treatment of Syphilis the old fashioned way with years of injections of not too effective drugs. As a sophomore medical student, I worked on the wards where we were using high fever induced typhoid vaccine to treat tertiary (Central Nervous System) syphilis.

Another sex related disease was gonorrhea. The Urology Clinic was inundated with male patients who in order to urinate needed frequent dilatations of their urethras with long filliform catheters. Antibiotics were not available to treat gonorrhea as they are today. After seeing these poor men, we did not want to be victims of syphilis or gonorrhea.

One skill that we learned in Dermatology and in Urology was prescription writing. We learned that the more elaborate the prescription the less likely it was effective.

In college I had 5 years of chemistry. The only course which I enjoyed was Analytical Chemistry, which involved the identification of unknown compounds. When I reached biochemistry in medical school, I finally found my great interest. The chemistry of the human body was fascinating. We were studying our own blood and urine and the lab tests we would use with patients.

Dr. Forbes, professor of Biochemistry, was an excellent teacher who believed in the importance of his subject. He also taught us to be skeptical of laboratory results and if the lab tests did not agree with our clinical judgment, to repeat the lab tests.

18. MEDICAL SCHOOL – SECOND YEAR

We did not have much patient contact as yet but we did begin Physical Diagnosis. This course was taught by Harry Walker, MD, the author of the textbook. He taught that in Physical Diagnosis, Inspection, Palpitation, Percussion and Auscultation were the blocking and tackling of the medicine game.

One day coming out of a patient's room, Dr. Walker stopped to talk to me. "I just examined this patient who has pneumonia", he said. "I told him that he was doing well and would recover completely". The patient told Dr. Walker that he (Dr. Walker) was the first doctor to reassure him that he would get better.

From then on I always told the child and the parents what was wrong with the child and that he or she would recover.

PSYCHIATRIC WARD JOB

At the end of our first year of medical school in June, 1942, we were informed that because our country was at war, the second year of school would begin immediately- no summer vacation. How was I to come up with the money for my second year? I asked for help from the medical school administration who found me a job working every 3rd night from 6 PM to 6 AM on the closed Psychiatric Ward. These were the same hours that I had worked as a bellboy at the Hotel Kimball the summer before.

My work on the Closed Psychiatric ward meant that not only were the patients locked in but so were the nurses and me. Most of the patients were not violent. We had one room with Tertiary Syphilis patients who were being treated with typhoid vaccine to induce high fever in an attempt to burn out the spirochetes in their brains and they could be troublesome.

We treated patients with schizophrenia. One modality was to wrap them in overlapping cold wet sheets. When we removed the sheets after 2-3 hours the sheets were warm. I doubt that this treatment helped any patient.

Since very few drugs were available, the only weapons the psychiatrists had were time, psychotherapy and sometimes shock therapy.

We were busy on the ward until midnight and after that I could sleep or study. The problem was that in the midst of psychotic patients, I had to be alert and yet I was too tired to study. As a result, the next day I was too tired to listen in class. I went from the top quarter of my class to the bottom. It did not occur to me to complain because I was in medical school and I was eating.

A SPECIAL GIRL

On Halloween night in 1942 a student dietitian friend brought her roommate along to scare me. They dressed in sheets and rang the bell on the Ward door. I wrote my mother that I had met the girl I wanted to marry. This is what I wrote in my diary on October 31, 1942: "I have had more than eight hours of sleep and the girl I met still looks better than any other I've met before. The problem is: how can I make a creature like her conscious of my existence. I'm going to try and if a miracle happens, I'll be the happiest man alive. She's what I've always imagined a heavenly creature is like, only she is real." November 14, 1942: "She's real and I've known her 15 days or 3 dates or 4 +5 + 7 = 16 hours. She dances like a dream. She can talk and she can listen. She's sincere. She's loyal. And she's beautiful. Heaven has opened a branch office here on earth."

19. MEDICAL SCHOOL –
FINAL TWO YEARS

At the end of my second year, I knew that once again we would continue on in school without a break. Many medical students had part-time jobs. Some of them lived lives of quiet desperation. A student friend one year ahead of me, committed suicide the day after his graduation. The Administrators of the Medical School were very kind in granting loans and allowing deferred payments— but I was still broke and worried.

Then a miracle happened. I was drafted as a private first class into the Medical Corps of the Army of the United States as were most of my classmates. Some students joined the Navy and we were all allowed to stay in Medical School.

The Army paid my tuition and all of my expenses. I had clothes— an Army uniform, shoes, books and food. I did not have to work and I could study full time. It was a miracle.

Being in the Army or Navy we were subject to all their rules and regulations. Army officers and enlisted men supervised the infrequent military classes and meetings we had to attend but generally they left us alone.

After receiving physical examinations at the old Belgian Building, which had been transferred from the 1939 New York World Fair, we started our third year of medical school.

Our social world was strange. On one hand we now had some money we could spend on dates, but on the other hand we were too busy studying to take advantage of our social opportunities. As future doctors we were good catches for the local girls as most other eligible young men were away in the Armed services.

Besides, I was interested in only one young lady. She was the one who had accompanied her roommate as a ghost to the Psychiatric Ward to scare me on Halloween. With my Army pay I could afford to take her out to dinner. She was at the Medical College of Virginia for a one-year dietetic internship. It took only a few dates for me to solidify my desire to marry her.

My medical school classmates and I were now beginning our clinical years. Compared to the first two basic years, these years seemed less stressful. Unless we really screwed up we would become doctors of medicine. We were still divided into teams of eight students. None of us were married. It was considered to be almost unethical to be married. Some hospitals, e.g. Strong Memorial Hospital in Rochester, N.Y., would not accept married interns.

As sophomore medical students, we knew everything. As junior medical students we were not so sure. We had classes in the Clinic Building Amphitheater but most of our work was in the Clinic or on the Hospital Wards.

One of my patients was an elderly gentleman who had been diagnosed as having heart disease. Because we were studying hiatal hernias, I ordered X-rays, which demonstrated that my patient had a hiatal hernia. For three months I was the great physician who had made a correct diagnosis until my patient died of heart disease.

I learned that a patient can have more than one disease. If a patient has one diagnosis and is not responding to the treatment, look for other diseases. If a newborn has one congenital anomaly, look for other anomalies. Years later a newborn with imperforate anus was referred to me from upper Michigan. I assured the referring physician that our surgeons could handle that problem. When the newborn arrived at our hospital, our exam revealed a tracheoesophageal fistula as well. We did not have a pediatric surgeon available. Our adult cardiac surgeon was able to repair the TE fistula beautifully. Both ends of the baby went home in good condition to the Michigan wilderness.

Obstetrics was one clinical experience that most of us dreaded. First, we had to memorize the complex route of the newborn down the birth canal. Second, we were taught in a manner that implied that we were stupid—which we probably were. Our instructor told us that we were the worst group he had ever tried to teach.

To balance the record, when our group was on the Pediatric Service, Dr. Lee Sutton, Chief of Pediatrics, labeled us "the best group I have ever taught". Six of our group of eight became Pediatricians. It is amazing what a little praise can do to improve performance.

We delivered our clinic patients in their homes. We went as a team: a student nurse, a junior medical student and a senior medical student. Even in the worst sections of Richmond, Virginia, our white uniforms seemed to protect us from harm. When we were on call for home deliveries, we had to be ready 24 hours a day.

Once when we delivered a baby in a very poor home, the father of the baby showed us a room full of clothes. His employer had given him all the clothes that either a boy or a girl would need from birth to the age of 12 years.

Often, either George Washington or Abraham Lincoln or one of our names was given to a baby we delivered.

Dr. Isaac Bigler was the Chief of Surgery and presented patients to us in the amphitheater. He often smoked a cigarette as he lectured. He died of cancer of the lung. How little we knew.

SENIOR YEAR

During our senior year several of us worked as externs at a small local hospital. One or two nights a week we did histories and physicals on patients and gave drop ether for obstetrical deliveries. It was good experience, the source of some income and it made us feel like doctors.

Near the end of our senior year we all took the Virginia State written examinations in basic sciences and clinical subjects to be licensed to practice medicine. The exams were easy for us then, but would be very difficult to pass today. All members of my class passed.

During my senior year, Jacques P. Gray, MD became the new Dean of the Medical School. He appointed representatives of each medical school class to advise him. I was chosen for our senior class.

GRADUATION

As the time for our September graduation approached, Dr. Gray called me to his office to discuss two of my classmates. Since our class was composed of only 75 members we knew each other well. The seniors he wished to discuss were ranked 74th and 75th in the class. The question, which faculty members were asking, was whether these two should be graduated.

It was wartime and not being graduated meant going on active duty as enlisted men possibly in active combat. I told Dr. Gray that one of the two was going to be a general practitioner in his hometown of Virginia and the other student was interested in Dermatology. My classmates had good impressions of both students and thought that they would be good doctors. We did not know whether we influenced the Dean's decisions but both students were graduated.

Medical College of Virginia had a Dental School, Pharmacy School, and Nursing School. We were notified by official letter whether or not we would be graduated. For those of us in Medical School, our letter read either: "Dear Mr." or "Dear Doctor". As soon as we ripped the letter open, we knew our fate.

I had survived Medical School with one suit and one pair of shoes. Thanks to the US Army I had a free ride for my last two 9-month years.

My total expenses for my first two years were:

Room	*$180 ($10/month)*
Food	*$540 ($1/day)*
Tuition	*$700 ($350/year)*
Books	*$320*
Instruments	*$320*

My only other expenses were for laundry and other small items. Two years of Medical School cost me a grand total of $2060.00 ($1030/year)

I had been dating Martha Lake Adams since we first met in October of my sophomore year. I did not have time or money to pursue her until the Army came along at the start of my junior year (March). She finished her one-year internship in September 1943 and left for a position as dietitian at the Neurological Institute of Columbia University in New York City.

We wrote letters to each other for the next few months but no magical moment happened until she sent me brownies for Valentine's Day in 1944. I was then a senior in Medical School and I could see my future for the first time. At my invitation she came to visit me in June and I asked her to marry me. Fortunately she said "Yes!"

We picked out an engagement ring for $100 squeezed out of my Army pay and she took the train back to Manhattan. We set the wedding date for September 24, 1944, the day after my graduation from Medical School. I would not see her again until our wedding day.

The summer months passed quickly. There was no air conditioning and I was reminded once again how warm Virginia summers could be. If you sat quietly and did nothing, the sweat still dripped off of you.

I applied and was accepted for a rotating internship at New York City Hospital on Welfare Island in New York City. The US Army Medical Corps would allow me detached duty for 9 months for the internship.

Graduation Day finally arrived. My class assembled near the Governor's Mansion and marched across the park to a downtown theater. The evening was cool and pleasant. After the usual religious and musical interludes we were awarded our Doctor of Medicine degrees. All of us then stood and pledged the Oath of Hipprocates. It was awesome. Also, most of us were commissioned as First Lieutenants in the Medical Corps of the Army of the United States.

My mother had come by train from Springfield, Massachusetts to be in the audience. She had supported me with love, money and pride. It was the proudest day of my life. A long journey was finished for both of us.

20. NEWLY MARRIED INTERN

The same night after graduation, my mother and I took the train to New York City. My suitcase with all my worldly possessions was missing on our arrival at Grand Central Station. By luck a taxi driver came back into the station carrying my bag, which had been placed in his trunk by mistake. My mother and I continued to Norwalk, Connecticut where I was married to Martha Lake Adams in the Congregational Church on the Green. After a reception (no liquor) at Martha's home on Dry Hill Road, we went by train to a honeymoon cottage in Danbury, Connecticut.

Our wedding was September 24th and I was due to start my internship on October 1. Since our time and our money were short, we aborted the honeymoon after two days and left for our apartment at 100 Haven Avenue around the corner from Columbia University Neurological Institute where my wife who was supporting us had to report as a dietitian at 6 AM each day.

To travel to the hospital from 100 Haven Avenue meant I had to take the A train on the subway from 168th Street to 59th Street, then ride the cross town trolley to the middle of the 59th Street Bridge, take the elevator to the ground level and walk a mile to the hospital along the East River. It took me one hour but I didn't mind.

NEW YORK CITY HOSPITAL

Our hospital with 900 beds was at one end of Welfare Island while Metropolitan Hospital was at the other end. The two hospitals covered the same central area of Manhattan. Each hospital alternated daily admissions. In other words, we admitted like crazy for 24 hours and then we had 24 hours to treat and study our patients. It was a system that worked well. Welfare Island was part of the Manhattan hospital system and included Bellevue Hospital to the south of our territory and Harlem Hospital to the north.

Our staff house was adjacent to the hospital surrounded on three sides by the East River and across from the site which later would be the United Nations. Ships, large and small passed by on an irregular basis.

There were 25 interns and 25 residents on the House Staff. One second or third year resident and one or two interns covered each ward. A ward had 34 beds all in one big room and all beds were full.

My income as an intern at New York City Hospital on Welfare Island was $35/month plus room, food and uniforms. The room was just that. It held a single cot, one bureau, and one window. The large bathroom was down the hall.

The food was not gourmet. Due to the war, we had no beef and no butter. We had plenty of chicken and eggs. It was too bad if we didn't like the food. We were on an island with no vending machines or stores and no other place to buy food or drink. Thin as I was from Medical School, I lost 10 more pounds during my internship.

On most Saturday nights an Attending Physician would supply a keg of beer. With a big Common Room and a pool table, being on call for the weekend was not too bad especially if my wife joined me.

On VE-Day, I called my wife at Columbia Neurological Institute that looked over the Hudson River to see if she had heard the news. The ships in both rivers were making so much noise we could not hear each other. It made for an exciting day.

We wore a white uniform with a red caduceus and "DH" for Department of Hospitals on the sleeve. We started each day with clean white shoes and uniforms but before the day was over, everything was dirty. Attending physicians from Columbia University and Flower 5th Avenue Medical Schools made rounds with their senior medical students. Priests from Maryknoll spent a year at the hospital before they went to China. Often I would be on one side of the bed and the priest would be on the other side.

Physicians and priests had a great relationship. As a critically ill heart attack patient lay between us, I would say, "You are not going to get this one!"

We were a charity hospital with no private rooms, no privacy, very few baths and no back rubs. There was only one nurse per 8 hour shift. The patients were the bums, prostitutes, and inhabitants of the tenements and some drunken policemen. With a saloon every few blocks and the temptation of the hospitable bartender, it was no wonder that we admitted many cops who had imbibed too freely. We never reported any of them. Would you?

We had no antibiotics, few sophisticated lab studies and very few X-rays. After hours and on weekends, the interns did the lab work and took the x-rays. The hours were long and our work was never finished but nothing stood between the patient and us. Doing a CBC late one night on an old ex-Broadway star, I saw some peculiar white cells on the blood smear. The cells were plasma cells and the patient had plasma cell leukemia, only the 12th case ever reported.

One weekend I must have x-rayed and set fractures on every long bone (except the femur) in the body. We gave morphine IV, set the bone and applied the cast.

CASES

A 19 year-old woman arrived at our ER bleeding in the first trimester of pregnancy. In medical terms she was having a threatened abortion. As we prepared to admit her, two detectives appeared. They demanded, "Who is threatening to abort this woman?" We explained to the policemen that the woman's body was threatening to abort.

We had one ward filled with prostitutes who had syphilis. We were giving them a new drug from Maxwell Finland of Boston. The drug was penicillin and we were giving it in 25,000 unit doses. Nowadays we know this amount was inadequate but we did not know that then.

The strengths of our rotating internship were the volume of patients and the quality of the attending staff. Dr. Babcock from Columbia University School of Medicine was the author of a four-volume Textbook of Surgery. As he made rounds one day with a group of medical students, when they tried to exam a patient, the patient said, "It's OK with me if it's OK with my doctor." They made a hurried search for me on the fringes of the group.

I told Dr. Babcock that I thought the patient had carcinoma of the stomach. His diagnosis was carcinoma of the colon because of the fresh blood in the stool. At surgery the lower abdominal incision and exploration revealed no colon cancer. The incision was extended upward where the stomach malignancy was discovered. My bible was Dr. Cope's "The Physical Diagnosis of the Acute Abdomen".

The incident taught me to have faith in my history and physical examination and to stand up for my diagnosis. It also taught me to listen to the student or interns in later years when I was the attending physician.

A.B. Cannon was the Chief Attending in Dermatology. He would arrive once a week from his Park Avenue office at 1 PM. Rumor had it that he always showered and changed his clothes before arriving and he looked it. He was accompanied by a group of lesser doctors.

At his first visit he would ask the intern's name and write the name in his little black book. At each subsequent visit he always addressed the intern by name. He then proceeded to one of the Dermatology wards where he and his seated doctors were presented patients for diagnosis and treatment. Patients and interns were always handled with dignity and courtesy. By example he taught us to be gentlemen.

"Whatsoever you do unto them, you do unto me".

On a cold snowy night in February, a 62-year-old man fell on a Manhattan Street and was brought to the hospital by ambulance. (I must explain. All our patients came by ambulance. We were on an island and nobody walked by our front door. We were thus spared the minor injuries and illnesses that a usual ER would receive). He complained of severe hip pain and could not move his leg. Our diagnosis was a possible fracture of the hip. As was our custom, we did not attempt to remove his many layers of clothing before taking x-rays of his hip. When we looked at the films, the cause of his discomfort was obvious. He had placed his dentures in his hip pocket and they had bitten him.

One Ward that was very busy in winter months was the Women's Orthopedic Ward. Hip fracture was the number one diagnosis. I became expert in putting these lovely ladies in traction where they remained for many months until their hips healed or they died of pneumonia. Hips were not pinned and pneumonia was common because of being confined in bed in a hospital where there was plenty of bacteria.

AUTOPSY
One of my first friends among the 50 interns and residents was Joe

Goldzieher, Pathology Resident. We did not have scans or MRI's and autopsies were often needed to find the cause of death. Daily we stopped in the Pathology Building to examine the gross autopsy specimens.

In those days, a hospital had to have an autopsy rate of at least 25% to be accredited. In other words, one out of every four deaths must have an autopsy. Autopsies were important to the doctor so that he would know why the patient died to prevent other patients from dying. It was also important that the family know why the patient died. The patient might have a contagious disease which could be dangerous for a family member or have a congenital defect that might appear later in a family member.

Whenever a death occurred, our duty was to obtain permission for an autopsy. This was often very difficult for religious or other reasons. I soon became very proficient at obtaining autopsy permission when other doctors failed. My reward was a night off call so I could go home to my wife.

To obtain an autopsy, I called on the family of the patient. If the body was already transferred to a funeral home before we received permission for the autopsy, Joe and I went to the funeral parlor to do the autopsy after we obtained permission.

WAS COLONEL DINSLAW A CON ARTIST OR NOT?

We wore many hats as interns at a big city hospital. One of our projects was helping the FBI. There was a con artist named Colonel Dinslaw. He had invented a machine which projected a different colored light on areas of the body to cure different diseases. Although he had been brought to trial several times, the case was always dismissed. No one else had tried the machine to prove it was worthless.

The FBI commissioned us to do a clinical trial. We chose patients in the chronic men's ward in the basement of the hospital. Most of these men had been in the hospital for weeks to months with very little attention paid to them. We chose patients with hypertension and in accordance with the inventor's instructions shone an ordinary light bulb with a red filter focused over their hearts. Much to our surprise most of the men's blood pressure dropped.

Was the drop in their blood pressure due to the red light or because someone was giving them kind attention? At any rate our results did not help the FBI.

This illustrated to me why and how whatsoever you do for a patient may work if you are kind and the patient has faith in you.

DRUGS

Many physicians from Europe were migrating to the United States because of World War II. Some of them were required to spend time at a US hospital in order to be licensed to practice medicine. One such doctor was Angelus Angelussuch, MD., Resident in ENT. He had been a leading specialist in Vienna, Austria.

I sought treatment from him when I developed a sinus infection. He used topical cocaine to numb my nose for a medical procedure. When I walked from the hospital to the staff house, I felt as if I were floating through the air with my feet 3 feet off the ground. For the first time I understood what it must be like to use cocaine. It was also the last time.

Drug addicts were not a major problem in our society then and those that lived in Manhattan were confined to a small area off Broadway north of 59th Street.

However, one evening a pregnant drug addict arrived at our ER. She was almost at term and wanted to be admitted with the hope of getting off drugs so that her baby might have a better chance to be normal. I admitted her to our maternity unit. The older doctors told me that I had made a mistake in admitting her. They said that every addict in Manhattan would be coming to our hospital for drugs. Contrary to their warning, no other addict arrived. She had her baby two weeks later and the baby and mother left the hospital in good condition.

CHILDREN'S WARD

We had a separate building for sick children. Each of the three floors had a large outdoor porch. The standard treatment for pneumonia was plenty of fresh air, weather permitting. The children were wheeled out on the porch daily. We had sulfonamides but no penicillin or other antibiotics. If parenteral fluids were needed, they were given subcutaneously – not IV.

Almost every child who was admitted had head and body lice. Before admission to the wards, each child's hair was deloused with kerosene and wrapped in a towel.

Children with contagious diseases were not admitted but instead were sent to Willard Parker Hospital. Each large city had a communicable disease hospital. These hospitals admitted Diphtheria, Whooping Cough, Chicken Pox, Poliomyelitis, Tuberculosis, etc. As a result the average doctor did not see any of these and therefore lacked the experience in this phase of his training.

In 1944-45 it was not common for hospital patients to have visitors. We were on an island not easily accessible to parents or other relatives. I do not remember a single visitor during my internship.

One item we had plenty of was flowers. At the end of each day, the funeral directors of Manhattan delivered the excess flowers to the city hospitals. Whenever, I went off duty to return to my wife, I always brought her a large bouquet of flowers.

The Jewish interns on our staff always covered for the Christian doctors over Christmas and we covered for them over Hanukkah. I remember leaving the hospital at 3 PM on December 24th, 1944 with my usual bouquet of flowers. I rode the trolley to the mainland at 59th Street. It was snowing lightly. People were rushing about. The Salvation Army Kettle Stand was playing "Silver Bells" and I was going home to my first Christmas with my new bride. I had stepped into a different world and even 56 years later it is my fondest memory of Christmas Eve.

SUMMARY

Would I recommend that any young doctor intern at a big city hospital today. If it was like ours I would say "NO". With 900 beds, the hospital was too big. There weren't enough nurses, aides, clerks, and other personnel so we did some of their work and most of the lab work. After hours and on weekends we took x-rays. Food was inadequate and there was no place to obtain food if we wanted it. The intern quarters and pay were substandard. Our income was $35.00 per month.

Why did we intern at New York City Hospital? We had been brought up on "Green Light" by C. Lloyd Douglas, "Of Human Bondage" by Somerset Maughm and the Dr. Kildare movies with Lew Ayres and Lionel Barrymore. Could we have done any differently?

Nothing can compare to the excitement of a new young doctor being immersed in the bizarre world of a big city charity hospital. The poverty and the difficulties only added to the glamour. Next to the months at Belmont (a communicable disease) Hospital, it was the most exciting time of my life.

On June 30, 1945, I rode the trolley onto the 59th Street mainland for the last time. It was 9 PM and the bums were already asleep in some of the storefronts. I was tempted to attach a tag to some of them welcoming the new group of interns to our club.

21. MEDICAL CORPS DUTY
IN WAR TIME

On July 1, 1945 I was assigned to active duty at the US Army Field Service School in Carlisle Barracks, Pennsylvania. Six weeks of training transformed us into Army Officers. At least we had the uniforms and the rank of First Lieutenant. The teaching was first class based on the principle of repeating everything five times. Then we received our assignments. I was sent to Cushing General Hospital in Framingham, Massachusetts.

ARMY SERVICE

During World War II there were General Hospitals in various areas of the United States. Each hospital was a center for different sorts of trauma. Cushing General Hospital was a Neurological Center and I was a Peripheral Nerve Injury Ward officer.

With a convoy of ambulances we met the incoming ambulance planes from the South Pacific at an airfield in Bedford, Massachusetts and transported the wounded soldiers to our hospital. My function was to diagnose and position the specific nerve injury and present the patient to the Neurosurgeons who operated to rejoin the nerves.

Each report began WIA (wounded in action). By testing the motor and sensory functions of the different peripheral nerves we usually could locate the nerve injury.

On the upper extremity we tested the following nerves: spinal accessory, dorsalis scapulae, long thoracic, thoraco dorsalis, pectoral, suprascapular, musculo cutaneous, axillary, radial, medial and ulnar.

On the lower extremity we checked the femoral, sciatic, posterior tibial and the common peroneal. Sometimes more than one nerve was damaged.

The most frequently injured nerve was the ulnar. The site of the wound was at the back of the elbow in the groove between the medial epicondyle of the humerus and the elecranon. The injury was usually due to shrapnel. The ulnar nerve separates from the brachial artery before reaching the elbow so that sometimes the artery is spared.

The least common peripheral nerve injury that we saw was the femoral because these cases usually died before we saw them. The femoral nerve in the inguinal area is so close to the artery that if it is hit, there is fatal blood loss. In my months at Cushing General I saw only one femoral nerve injury.

Without "Peripheral Nerve Injuries—Principles of Diagnosis" by Webb Haymaker and Barnes Woodhall, I could not have functioned as a Peripheral Nerve Injury ward Officer. Although I did not realize it at the time of my wartime nerve injury experience, what I learned was very valuable during polio epidemics in later years.

OUR SON IS BORN AT FORT MONMOUTH, NEW JERSEY

My next assignment was at Fort Monmouth Regional Hospital in Red Bank, New Jersey. My job description was to assist in the discharge of General Patton's Armored Column of 55,003 enlisted men and 6,509 officers.

During the discharge physical examination (not performed by me) anyone who needed further evaluation was sent to my two 48-bed Holdover Barracks. I had 48 hours to determine whether the individual soldier needed to be sent to an Army Hospital or could be discharged from the Army.

We did a history and physical examination on each new arrival. Then we treated the man for scabies with benzyl benzoate. Scabies was not the reason these soldiers were sent to us but while we had them we treated them— and they were grateful.

Our Holdover buildings received 411 soldiers, 53 officers, and 388 enlisted men from September 29, 1945 to February 4, 1946. No disease was found on 167. We hospitalized 138 for further study. In those we hospitalized the diseases ranged from high blood pressure to glomerulonephritis, tuberculosis, gastric and duodenal ulcers, hemorrhoids, inguinal hernia, deafness, infected scabies and syphilis.

Many soldiers complained of chest pain. We were very aware of "Soldier's Heart" of World War I and we did not want to make a cardiac cripple out of a normal soldier. After a careful history and examination and a normal EKG, a full explanation was given to the patient. If he still seemed worried, I arranged to be called out of the room and left the EKG report with its "NORMAL" reading on my desk in his view.

Our son, Garwood Elliott, was born at Fort Monmouth Regional Hospital on January 8, 1946. Because I was in the Army, the only expense was a $25 War Bond that I gave to the obstetrician.

22. BELLE MEADE GENERAL DEPOT

My next and last assignment was at Belle Meade General Depot in Belle Meade, New Jersey. My official title was Depot Surgeon and I provided medical services to 30 Quartermaster officers, 10,000 civilian workers and 5000 German Prisoners of War.

For the Army officers and civilians I had a dispensary with nurses, pharmacist and an x-ray technician. I conducted sick call each day and handled accidents and illnesses as they occurred. Because most of the employees were women, I soon became an expert on dysmenorrhea. My practice was as a general practitioner with a few strange twists.

A German Medical Corps Unit held sick call in German with me each morning for the German prisoners of war. The PW's slept in a stockade behind barbed wire and worked in the Depot during the day. As far as I know, no prisoner tried to escape. Why should they?

I explained to my enlisted men that we were not at war with the PW's. If we wanted the American PW's to be treated well in Germany then we would treat the German PW's humanely. One PW developed manic-depressive psychosis and I sent him to a military psychiatric hospital.

When my daughter Robin was a senior in high school, we had an exchange student from Hilden, Germany. Her name was Annette Juntgen and her father, Max, was a German fighter pilot who was shot down over England and spent the rest of World War II as a PW there. When my wife and I visited Max in Hilden 25 years after the war, he took us for a ride in his plane.

My responsibilities also included sanitation of the Depot grounds and restaurant. I made an inspection tour each month with a written report to the Commanding Colonel. The Depot was the supply area for the New York Port of Embarkation and the inspection took all day. I knew better than anyone else where everything was.

As the war was drawing to a close, surplus items were being sold. Jeeps were being sold for $600 and I applied to buy one. I was informed that none were left. I drove the civilian officials to the area where there were 200 Jeeps in crates. I never did get my jeep.

Six months after arriving at Belle Meade Depot, I added another smaller Dispensary at a Supply Depot in Somerville, 6 miles away.

Because there was a doctor shortage during the war, I made house calls to the civilian and Army children in the area. When my pharmacist and x-ray technician left I assumed their duties as well.

The German PW's were sent back to Germany shortly after V-E day. I gave some medical supplies to my German Corpsmen because I knew that they would face difficult times and shortages in Germany.

We took our six month old son, Gary, to Charles Hendee Smith, MD, a pediatrician in New Brunswick, New Jersey. I called Gary "Smoky" because as he was trying to wake up he made noises like a choo-choo train and we knew he would be crying soon for food. Dr. Smith had tears in he eyes when he said that was what he called his son too.

Dr. Smith had retired as Chief of Staff at New York University Department of Pediatrics before practicing in New Brunswick. He was a wonderful gentleman and very kind to us. Years later he wrote and wanted me to join him in his practice. I wish I could have.

After a year at Belle Meade, I was promoted to Captain in the Medical Corps in the Army of the United States. Life was pleasant. I had an Army car, two dispensaries with nurses, a pharmacy and x-ray equipment and thousands of generally healthy patients. It was difficult to depart the Army which had been my existence for most of 5 years. My patients sent me a letter thanking me for being their doctor and wishing me the best. My Army medical assignments had all been in the United States. Each hospital, Cushing General Hospital, Fort Monmouth Regional Hospital and Belle Mead General Depot taught me different aspects of medical care and I was a full time doctor in each of them.

23. PEDIATRIC RESIDENCY TRAINING

PETER BENT BRIGHAM HOSPITAL, BOSTON, MASSACHUSETTS

With 40,000 discharged Medical officers looking for Residency training positions, it was difficult to find a vacant slot. When no Pediatric Residency opening seemed available, Dr. Thomas Kinney offered me a position at Peter Bent Brigham Hospital in Boston in pathology.

After I agreed to go to Boston with Dr. Kinney, I received an offer from Children's Hospital in Washington, D.C. However, I felt committed to Dr. Kinney and did not feel that I could accept the offer. Additionally, I felt that the exposure to great physicians of Boston was an opportunity I could not miss.

To illustrate the Boston doctor's view of the United States, I relate this true example. Kenneth Sands, M.D. was a neurology resident at Boston Children's Hospital under Bronson Carothers, M.D. Dr. Sands traveled over many areas of the United States looking for a place to practice. Upon returning, he dutifully reported that one could not practice good medicine more than 35 miles from Boston.

About a year later, Charles A. Janeway, Chief of Staff, interviewed me for a residency at Children's Hospital. He said, "If you had gone to a first class medical school or had a first class internship we might consider you" (meaning around Boston). Both my medical school and my internship had been more that 35 miles from Boston.

We moved into a fourth floor walk-up apartment in Roxbury, Massachusetts two blocks from Peter Bent Brigham Hospital. I returned to that neighborhood ten years later and was afraid to walk around in broad daylight. Our apartment had an ice box, no refrigerator, no air conditioning. The ice man climbed three flights of stairs to replenish our ice every few days. It was the hottest summer of the decade. I had no rank, no status, no car and no civilian clothes. Under the GI bill I received $90 each month. So my wife went to work for a few months as a dietitian at Peter Bent. Her grandmother came to care for our eighteen-month-old son.

At the Brigham, I did autopsies and processed slides in a gigantic carousel that required 24-hour servicing. After the gross anatomy dissection we took sections of significant organs from which we made slides for microscopic study. A total gross and microscopic autopsy took 30 to 40 hours. Did I enjoy doing autopsies? NO! But it was a great way to re-learn anatomy, a fact I did not appreciate at the time.

I presented gross specimens and projected slides to Dr. Samuel Levine's Cardiology group. Dr. Levine was the author of "Clinical Heart Disease" and each summer had a month long course in Cardiology attended by 40 to 50 family doctors. He was an outstanding teacher but he had the habit of trailing off at the end of each sentence.

One morning in July, 1947 a 19 year old sailor's body was brought to the autopsy room after just having died on the operating table. As I was beginning the autopsy, a short surgeon in a white coat over his surgical scrubs appeared and began to diagram on the blackboard what had happened at surgery. The sailor had coarctation of the aorta. When the surgeon began manipulating the aorta, some of the friable intercostal arteries began to bleed and the bleeding could not be controlled. The surgeon spoke calmly, not with arrogance or with sorrow, but with a scientist's interest in knowing that what he had learned at surgery and what he would learn at autopsy could save many lives in the future.

The surgeon (I later learned) was Robert E. Gross who was the William E. Ladd Professor of Children's Surgery, Chief of Surgical Service at Children's Hospital, Boston. Three years later, in 1950, he reported on "Coarctation of the Aorta, Surgical Treatment of One Hundred Cases". His book, "The Surgery of Infancy and Childhood" was published in 1953. I bought one of the first copies and it sits on my desk as I write.

Another autopsy was on Elliott C. Cutler, M.D. who had been Chief of Surgery at the Brigham before he became the Chief Surgical Consultant for the European Theater of War. I knew him only as a body in the autopsy room. However, I thought he must be important because Dr. S. Burt Wolback, Chief of Pathology at Peter Bent Brigham was present. Dr. Wolback made the first chest incision and then handed the knife to me. As I remember, Dr. Cutler had carcinoma of the prostate with metastases to the lumbar vertebrae.

While doing another autopsy on a patient who had tuberculosis, I made a slide that showed tuberculosis and carcinoma in the stomach. The current medical opinion was that the two diseases could not coexist.

The Brigham had a lunchroom and we could eat great food and sit at a table and converse with physicians who were world renown. I noticed what busy Dr. Kinney chose for lunch. It usually consisted of only a cold sandwich and warm pop. I thought I would never dine as he did but as I became very busy in my practice, I was lunching the same way.

While in Boston, I had learning experiences with each of these Boston Physicians: John Enders, Sidney Farber, Charles Janeway, Lewis Webb Hill, John Homans, Nathan Talbot, Allen Butler, Victor Vaughn, Fuller Albright, George W. Thorne, Robert Gross, Bronson Carothers, Orvar Swenson, Sydney Gellis, Joseph Garfield, Louis K. Diamond, Samuel Levine and Clement Smith.

I attended many sessions that Dr. Janeway conducted in the amphitheater at Children's Hospital.

For Dr. Diamond and other doctors, I twice showed the slides for a two-week review course at Massachusetts General Hospital. Lewis Webb Hill, then the world authority on skin disease in children, allowed me to attend his Eczema Clinic each week. Victor Vaughn taught me how to do a replacement transfusion in a Hess incubator.

Bronson Carothers presented some unusual appearing children at a teaching session at Children's Hospital one morning and I found my attention wandering. I did not believe that I would ever see these children in my practice. However, in my first year as a pediatrician, I saw three different children with this syndrome: Hurler's Disease, also known as Gargoylism. I recognized these children immediately because of that demonstration by Dr. Carothers.

Sydney Gellis was in charge of the Outpatient Clinics at Children's Hospital and led a number of discussions. James Garland, who was Editor of the New England Journal of Medicine, gave lectures in the Ether Dome at MGH.

Dr. Fuller Albright was the authority on calcium metabolism. A retarded 5-year-old boy came in with what looked like a calcium stone in his bladder. Dr. Albright held the x-ray film up to the light. Dr. Albright was already exhibiting signs of Parkinson's Disease. With shaky hands and shaky voice, he said, "It looks like a shoe string to me". He was correct. This mentally retarded boy had threaded a shoestring through his urethra into his bladder.

Dr. Sidney Farber, the Chief of Pathology at Children's Hospital was working on leukemia in children which was then almost 100% fatal. Dr. Rudolph Toch joined him a few years later.

George W. Thorne was the Professor of the Theory and Practice of Physic at Harvard University School of Medicine and Chief of Medicine at Peter Bent Brigham. Hospital. He wrote a paper "The Physiological Basis for the Treatment of Nephritis" which was published in the New England Journal of Medicine. There were many children who developed acute glomerulonephritis as a sequela of rheumatic fever. Because of that one article, I never lost a child with glomerulonephritis.

MASSACHUSETTS GENERAL HOSPITAL, BOSTON

After 3 months at Peter Bent Brigham, an opportunity arose for a Fellowship in Pediatrics at Massachusetts General Hospital under Dr. Allen Butler. Dr. Butler was Chief of Pediatrics and Nathan Talbot was his assistant. Dr. Butler initiated the Ross Laboratory Conferences, which were published and sent to all pediatricians in the United States and Canada. He was a rebel and advocated many changes in medical philosophies, which later came to pass.

Dr. Talbot was a perfectionist who was in command of the lecture room from the room temperature to the lighting to the window shades to the length of the presentations.

He was the mentor whom I tried to copy in teaching Family Practice Residents for 50 years.

HARVARD-DEVENS HOUSING, AYER, MASSACHUSETTS

With the change from the Brigham to MGH there was opportunity to move from Roxbury to Harvard-Devens Village in Ayer, Massachusetts. The Village was formerly the barracks for Ft. Devens converted into family housing for Harvard students. Our living standard improved but there was a mile walk to the railroad station, a 40-minute train ride and a 10-minute walk to MGH. One advantage was that I became the pediatrician to all the families at Harvard-Devens Village and I could make my house calls through the connecting corridors of the housing Project.

With a 2-year-old son and a pregnant wife, my $90 monthly check from the Veteran's Education Fund was not enough. The additional income from the house calls helped. I was not paid directly by the families but through the Mt Auburn Medical Center, a cooperative devised by Dr. Allen Butler and MGH. The plan provided low cost medical care for Harvard student families and it worked well for me. I usually made my sick calls in the evening or on weekends after returning from MGH.

Although few people had cars in those post-war years, I occasionally managed a car ride to Boston instead of taking the train. Automobiles were few because cars had not been manufactured during the war and most people could not afford them if they were available.

When my wife went into labor with our second child, the Village Housing Manager drove her to Essex House at MGH. Our daughter, Robin McWilliams, named after my mother, was one of the first rooming-in newborns, i.e. she stayed in the same room with her mother at Phillips House at MGH. The rooming-in confused the business office. They presented me with a bill for nursery occupancy. I explained that my daughter did not occupy the nursery. Another bill was for formula. I said, "My daughter was breast fed". Our total hospital bill came to $30. Dr. Bacon, the obstetrician, did not charge for the delivery because those were the days of professional courtesy.

I never charged for my medical care rendered to doctors' children.

MASSACHUSETTS GENERAL HOSPITAL

In January 1948, we had the opportunity to move to Harvard Housing in Cambridge, across the highway from The Charles River. Friends with a car drove my wife, 2-year old Gary, 2-month old Robin and our dog to Cambridge.

I rode in a pickup truck with all our possessions, which consisted of only one double mattress and box springs, 2 bunk beds from the Army, one sofa, one green bookcase, 4 straight chairs, one table and one portable crib.

Our housing was in a multiple one story barracks type unit with an oil drum in front. Heat was provided by a space heater which had to be periodically filled with kerosene. The unit had bare floors, single pane windows, no storm windows and no storm door. I still remember how cold it was even after I filled and lit the space heater.

Lytt Gardner, who later became Chief of Pediatrics at State University of New York Upstate Medical Center in Syracuse, lived two doors away. When one of his children was born at Essex House, he did femoral vein sticks on the baby to obtain blood for his calcium studies. He lived in fear that his wife would find out what he was doing to their newborn.

Two colleagues, Katie Kiehl, MD and Berry Brazelton, MD, also Fellows in Pediatrics at MGH, and I would walk to Katie Kiehl's apartment behind Massachusetts General Hospital where she fed us potato soup for lunch. Then she took us in her car to the clinic at 69 Battle St., in Cambridge, Massachusetts to see patients. Dr. Brazelton became famous as a developmental pediatrician with many books and television programs.

BOSTON MEDICINE

This was the time of electrolytes and fluid balance. The second edition of James L. Gambles's "Chemical Anatomy, Physiology and Pathology of Extracellular Fluid" had just been published. Dr. Allen Butler and his associates were formulating their initial hydrating solution and their maintenance fluids. IV fluids were beginning to replace subcutaneous fluids. There were basic rules. First, prime the kidney with a glucose-hypotonic saline solution. Second, give no potassium until you are certain that the kidneys are working. How do you know that the kidneys are working? Wait for the child to urinate. In spite of all the elaborate calculations, Dr. Gamble said, "If the kidneys are working, you are a hero. If they are not, you are a bum".

We also spent much time in studying the treatment of diabetic acidosis and coma, which has much to do with fluids and electrolytes.

We had many discussions around the big conference table in Dr. Butler's office with professors from MIT. One of the sad events of World War II and the Post-War years was the death of a father and the realization by his children that their father would never be coming home. During the war years when I was receiving casualties from the South Pacific, I was too involved with medical details to have many philosophical thoughts. In retrospect, I am horrified at the wounding and killing of millions of men and women in war.

Most of my contemporary friends were in the service in World War II. When I went to my 50th high school reunion, the pictures of my classmates who had been killed during the war were posted on the wall. I felt guilty and thankful that I had survived. I thought of the 50 years of life that I had enjoyed while they had not. Their sacrifice was for my children and me.

In 1947-48 when I was at MGH the thought was that we must keep the Pediatric Wards sanitary. Parents were only allowed to visit was on Sunday afternoons between 2-4 PM and in the meantime, if we wanted to talk to them we had to go downstairs to the lobby. The Germans had similar thinking. When I visited the Children's Hospital in Amsterdamer Strasse in Munich, Germany in 1963, parents were not allowed inside the hospital. They had to stand on an outside balcony to see and talk with their children via intercom. How times have changed.

MGH had a 50 bed Emergency Room Ward. Any patient who came to the ER could be treated and sent home or be admitted to the ER Ward for no longer than 48 hours and then either discharged or admitted to the hospital. Morning rounds were therefore first made in the ER. Bedside rounds on the Pediatric Wards then followed.

We attended the weekly Clinicopathological Exercises that were also published in the New England Journal of Medicine. This was exciting to actually be present at an event that I had read about for years in the Journal.

24. PEDIATRIC RESIDENCY IN
THE WILDERNESS

By the time I finished at MGH, there were still thousands of ex-Medical Officers scrambling for residency training programs. However, an opportunity opened at Central Maine General Hospital in Lewiston, Maine. Dr. Glidden Brooks, who had been Chief Resident at Boston Children's Hospital had established an approved program at CMG.

There are three large regional hospitals in Maine: Maine General in Portland, Central Maine General, and Eastern Maine General in Bangor. Together these three hospitals cover the state and were part of an outreach program associated with Boston University School of Medicine.

Thanks to a program that allowed ex-service men to have a priority, we bought our first automobile, a Chevrolet Malibu, for $1441. We loaded everything we owned into the car and drove to Lewiston. We rented an apartment in a French-speaking house. Soon our 2 year old son was speaking French almost better than English.

The first patient that I examined in Maine was a 2 year old boy who had a sore throat for 36 hours. He had respiratory distress with a grayish friable membrane on both tonsils. He was drooling. In common with many Maine children, he had received no immunizations. He had diphtheria. We gave him 20,000 units of diphtheria antitoxin and started him on penicillin. A tracheostomy was done three hours after admission. He received three doses of diphtheria antitoxin in the next two days. His throat culture grew Corynebacterium Diphtheria. Six days after admission, his EKG showed evidence of myocarditis. On the 7th day he had serum sickness with generalized urticaria. After 3 negative throat cultures he was discharged 30 days after admission.

Harriet was a 10 year old girl who had developed rheumatic heart disease at the age of three but no one had placed her on prophylactic penicillin. She developed mitral valve disease. We placed her on daily oral penicillin and scheduled regular check-ups. She would need valve replacement in the future.

We had many patients with either rheumatic fever or glomerulonephritis. These diseases are sequelae of streptococcal infections because the children were not treated with penicillin when they had strep throat. Children with rheumatic fever were usually not very sick but some developed mitral valve problems. We saw no chorea. We treated them with aspirin and bed rest.

KEROSENE

Patricia was the first of what would be a common admitting diagnosis. She was a 3 year old girl who began coughing after she had drunk a glass of kerosene one hour before admission. Chest x-rays showed the typical pneumonitis caused by the kerosene. Her hemoglobin was only 7.4 gms. She was placed on penicillin and iron and discharged home after 10 days in the hospital.

Kerosene was the fuel used to heat many of the homes and was stored in the oil drums, which had a can or bottle under the nozzle to catch the drippings. A thirsty child would drink the kerosene out of the can or bottle and become our guest with pneumonitis. We used penicillin or other antibiotics but I am not sure that they were of any help. Often the children were anemic or malnourished before coming to us.

THE BOY WHO WOULD RUN THE FAMILY STORE

Two weeks after I arrived in Maine, a 5 week old male infant was admitted in the morning. He had been sick since only 9 PM the night before when he refused his bottle. His alert family doctor sent the baby to the hospital. The family came from a small crossroads town where they ran a general store. They had 4 girls and this was the first male offspring. They needed him to continue the family store.

The infant had a slight fever and was irritable. His anterior fontanelle was not tense but he did not like to bend his neck so we did a lumbar puncture. His spinal fluid was cloudy and showed gram positive diplococci on smear. The culture grew pneumococcus Type I. In 1948 the chance of survival for a 5 week old male infant with pneumococcic meningitis was not very good. In his favor was the fact that the infant had not been sick very long. Louis Weinstein had just published a paper outlining the latest treatment, which was 25,000 units of penicillin IM every 4 hours and 10,000 units intrathecally once each day. We started treatment immediately.

Each day I did a lumbar puncture and gave him an injection of 10,000 units of penicillin mixed in saline solution. He was also given the 25,000 units of penicillin IM every 4 hours. The infant remained irritable and lethargic even though he was on IV fluids. He was stable but remained critical. On the 13th day or his illness, I gave him his penicillin intrathecally as usual at 9 AM. At 10:30 AM he began to convulse. The student nurse who had mixed the penicillin came to me and said, "I made a mistake". I mixed 100,000 units of penicillin instead of 10,000 units". I knew that she might be removed from the Nursing School if I reported what had happened. I said to her, "This will be our secret".

In spite of sedation the convulsions lasted for 4 hours. The infant then seemed more alert and started acting hungry for the first time. He improved rapidly during the next week. His spinal fluid became clear and grew no bacteria. He was discharged home 30 days after admission as well as any 2 month old infant.

How do I account for the good outcome? Did the infant finally receive a sufficiently high dose of penicillin? Good nursing care? Luck? Divine intervention? As far as I know this patient is still running a General Store somewhere in Central Maine. The lesson the nurses and I learned was:

Never ever give up!

APPENDICITIS

Appendicitis was often the cause of tummy pain of patients sent to the hospital. The first patient was a 15 yearold boy who had a gangrenous appendix but no peritonitis. The next child was not so lucky. He was a 10 year old boy whose appendix had perforated resulting in peritonitis. Although penicillin was the only antibiotic available, he responded well and was home in 10 days.

CAMPERS

It was summer in Maine and many children descended on the Maine camps. We never had a serious illness among the campers but we became expert in convincing parents hundreds of miles away that those of us in the wilderness were capable of providing adequate care for their sick or injured children.

Robert required tetanus antitoxin because of a buttocks laceration one week before and now appeared with generalized hives. He had a mild serum sickness secondary to the antitoxin and responded well to epinephrine injections and Benadryl.

TETANUS

Gerald was admitted August 11th with difficulty opening his mouth and rigid abdominal muscles. A diagnosis of presumptive tetanus was made and he was given 20,000 units of tetanus antitoxin IM after a negative skin test. Except for hives, which arrived one week later, his jaws and abdominal muscles relaxed and he was sent home after he was immunized with tetanus toxoid.

POLIOMYELITIS?

The first child with presumed poliomyelitis came in on July 31st. Laurier had a headache and stiff neck with lymphocytes, normal sugar and elevated protein in his spinal fluid. He spent two weeks in the hospital and recovered completely. Even though we diagnosed him with poliomyelitis, I doubt he had it. At that time we could not do viral studies on blood and stools to make an accurate diagnosis. Today, we can be more specific. The only evidence we had at that time was lymphocytic pleocytosis in the spinal fluid. Laurier probably had a viral encephalitis. The other viruses common to this are Mumps, Coxsackie, ECHO and Polio.

Our first real polio patient arrived September 23rd. He was a 16 year old boy with weakness of both lower extremities. During his 6 weeks in the hospital he was treated with hot packs and was improved at the time of discharge.

In September we also admitted a 14 year old boy with bulbar polio. He had paralysis of his palate and could not swallow his saliva. He learned to use an aspirating tube so that a tracheostomy was not necessary. The foot of his bed was kept elevated to facilitate draining of his mucus. He needed to remain hospitalized for two months and he made a complete recovery except for a slight residual huskiness of his voice. Bulbar polio patients often recover completely.

ACCIDENTS

Head injuries were common due to farm and field accidents. Eldon was 14 year old boy who was found lying unconscious in a field. He had been driving a team of horses that went out of control and he was thrown. He was comatose on admission with a laceration of his scalp. His skull x-rays showed no fracture. He remained unconscious for 4 days and required restraints for restless behavior. He was profane in his language. (This was common in children recovering from a severe head injury). His brain and general condition improved and in 10 days after the accident he went home.

We had no brain scan or MRI to assist our visualization of the brain and no Decadron to reduce intracranial pressure. Today the diagnosis would be easier and the duration of illness might be shorter.

The father of a 3 year old boy backed his truck over his son's head. The truck was moving slowly, the tire was a little flat and pushed the boy's head down into the mud. When we cleaned the mud off, the boy seemed normal except for a 2-inch laceration over his left eyebrow extending upward into his scalp. Skull x-rays were normal. We sutured his laceration, gave him a tetanus antitoxin shot and started him on penicillin. One week later he went home 100% all boy again.

An 8 month old infant was admitted because a car hit her carriage which was being pushed by her mother along the main highway. Some of us were suspicious that the mother was trying to kill her baby. Sure enough, six months later the baby was admitted again with same accident along the same road- only this time the baby died.

A 7 year old boy came into the ER at 6:30 PM after having been shot with a 22 long rifle bullet 30 minutes before. At surgery we found two holes in the jejunum, an injury to the liver and the edge of the right kidney with much retroperitoneal bleeding. Dr Twaddle was the surgeon and he exteriorized a double loop of small intestine for a colostomy. Blood transfusions, penicillin, streptomycin and tetanus antitoxin were given. The boy was admitted on 8/26/48 and the colostomy was closed on 12/10/48. He was able to go home two days before Christmas with an ample supply of toys. His family was very poor and hospital insurance was unknown then. The boy's mother was very grateful that her son had survived and she wanted to reward us. She said, "A big buck deer comes to our pond and I can show you where to sit to shoot him". I knew that the deer might represent the family's meat supply for the winter. I thanked her and declined her offer. Besides, I couldn't shoot a deer.

The people of Maine whose children we admitted to our hospital were honest, proud and very poor.

GLOMERULONEPHRITIS

Percylene was a 6 year old girl who had scarlet fever two weeks before Christmas. Her doctor treated her with sulfonamides but she continued to not feel well for several weeks. On 12/31/48 she was admitted unconscious. Her blood pressure was 170/120. Her urine had a specific gravity of 1.010 with 4 plus albumin, cloudy with many red blood cells. She had acute glomerulonephritis with hypertensive encephalopathy. Sometimes these children go blind until their blood pressure drops. She was given 4 cc. of 50% magnesium sulfate IM and this dose was repeated every 4 hours as needed during the next few days. She was also placed on phenobarbital. Her BP gradually returned to normal over the next 7 days. Her fluids were restricted to a maintenance level. Her urine cleared of red blood cells and her kidneys worked well. Improvement was slow but she finally went home on bed rest on 2/1/49.

Barbara was a 12 year old girl with acute hemorrhagic glomerulonephritis. This disease is a sequela of streptococcic pharyngitis. Children present with a bloody urine and high blood pressure. Most children with this illness recover completely. Death is not caused by high blood pressure or by high BUN but can be caused by heart failure or high blood potassium. At first we controlled the high blood pressure by giving various antihypertensive drugs. We kept the fluid intake at maintenance level so as not to overload the heart. We restricted potassium intake until the kidneys worked well enough to excrete the potassium. Barbara and her kidneys recovered completely but she had to stay six long weeks in the hospital.

Nephritis in our area was much more frequent than rheumatic fever. The children were very ill with high blood pressure and hypertensive encephalopathy but they usually made a complete recovery.

MENINGITIS

In January, we received a 6-month-old female infant with hemophilus influenza Type B meningitis. She was treated with sulfadiazine and streptomycin and was home in two weeks.

RICKETS

Between 1/15/49 and 3/16/49 four infants from six to ten months of age were admitted for various reasons and were diagnosed as also having rickets. All four drank milk, no solid foods and took no vitamins. In the cold sunless winter Maine months they had no source of Vitamin D. One infant broke his femur when his brother fell on him. The bone probably broke because it was weakened with rickets. Another infant's skull could be pressed inward like a ping pong ball. Another child had the characteristic rachitic rosary of his ribs. All x-rays revealed flaring and irregularity of the metaphyseal ends of the long bones.

All infants were given 10 drops of oleum percomorphus (vitamin D) three times a day and sent home on iron and an appropriate diet. Follow up exams and x-rays showed healing of the rickets. I wrote an article about the infants with rickets which was published in the Journal of the Maine Medical Association. My purpose was to alert the Maine doctors that rickets still existed and could easily be prevented. If our hospital had 4 infants with rickets how many more must be out there who have never been diagnosed?

DIABETES

In April, we admitted a 12 year old girl in diabetic coma. Her blood sugar was 600 mgms. We gave her insulin and IV fluids and brought her out of the coma and acidosis promptly. It was obvious that the girl's blood sugars had not been properly controlled for a long time.

FIRST REPLACEMENT TRANSFUSION IN MAINE

An infant was born to an RH-negative mother and he became jaundiced and needed a replacement transfusion. Victor Vaughn had taught me the procedure at Boston Children's Hospital. A replacement transfusion seemed easy to do in a Medical Center with all sorts of support but to do one in the wilderness would not be easy. What if the baby died?

The decision was easy. The infant needed the replacement now or he would die. We cross matched the correct RH negative blood and assembled our 3 way stopcock, plastic newborn feeding tube, other needed instruments and calcium. The procedure took 3 hours but we completed the first replacement transfusion in the State of Maine. The baby lived and went home a few days later.

There was never an empty bed on the Pediatric Ward. We made additional space on our enclosed sun porch, in the treatment room and broom closet.

The illnesses in Maine were different than in New York City. We admitted many children with orthopedic problems caused by neglect and delay. Torticollis had to be corrected surgically in 3, 7, and 9 year olds. Slipped capital femoral ephiphsis and aseptic necrosis of the femoral head were treated long after the diagnosis should have been made.

Rheumatic fever was found but often was over-diagnosed. Immunizations were not given. Diphtheria and tetanus were still around. Tetanus antitoxin was often followed by serum sickness 7-10 days later. Appendicitis was common and often not diagnosed until the appendix had ruptured. Head injuries were common due to farm or highway accidents. Accidental swallowing of kerosene resulted in pneumonitis or pneumonia. Forty-two children sick enough with bacterial pneumonia were admitted during the year. Pneumonia was often a complication of measles.

Christmas season was our happy time of the year. Since most of our patients at Central Maine General Hospital were very poor, we conspired to keep them in the hospital a few days longer during the holidays so that Santa Claus could visit them. Thanks to many social agencies and stores we had several rooms full of toys and other presents to distribute. Many of the children would receive little more than what we gave them.

CLINICS AROUND MAINE

An adjunct of our hospital duties was to attend the Maine Crippled Children's Services Clinics in various locations. For attending each Clinic I received $25 plus mileage and one free meal. Since my income as a Hospital Resident Physician was only $50/month attending a Clinic was good additional income.

At a clinic in Bangor at Eastern General Hospital, I examined 6 children who had been diagnosed as having rheumatic fever. Each child had been on bed rest for 6-12 months. When we examined them, they had a normal physical examination and nothing in their histories could support a diagnosis of rheumatic fever. A cardiologist who also examined the children agreed with me. We told the parents of these children that we did not know whether their children ever had rheumatic fever but they were well now and could get out of bed and be normally active.

Lesson: Do not label a patient with a disease without adequate evidence.

A similar problem existed when I began practice in South Bend, Indiana. A prominent family with two children who were my patients told me that they had another child who was not living with them. Both parents had been in the Armed Services during World War II. All three children lived with their grandparents during the last year of the war. Six year old Thomas became ill and was diagnosed with Rheumatic Fever by an internist and placed on bed rest. When his parents came home from the war, Thomas remained with his grandparents to be sure that had a quiet environment. I received and evaluated the EKG, lab and x-ray studies done on Thomas. None of these supported the diagnosis of rheumatic fever. His physical examination was normal. I recommended to his parents that they bring Thomas home and let him lead a normal life.

One way to get a reputation as a great physician is to give patients diseases they do not have – and then cure them. Once a physician has given a disease to a patient it may be very difficult to take the disease away.

25. CONTAGIOUS DISEASE RESIDENCY

As I was finishing my year at Central Maine General Hospital, I realized that I had little training in contagious diseases. I called Louis Weinstein M.D., Chief of Haynes Memorial Hospital, a contagious disease hospital in Brighton, Massachusetts where I had attended his Saturday morning infectious disease lectures. He told me of an opening at Belmont Hospital in Worcester, Massachusetts. I applied and was accepted

Between 1860 and 1920 the serious infectious diseases were typhoid fever, tuberculosis and pneumonia. There were also epidemics of diphtheria, scarlet fever and measles. Little could be done to treat these diseases and hospital care was largely custodial. Despite the availability of vaccination, small pox was still around with a mortality rate of 24-30%

At first these diseases were treated in separate contagious wards in general hospitals. In 1890 the thought of treating these diseases away from the general hospitals was developed. Accordingly separate contagious disease hospitals were built. The first of these were six: South Department of Boston City Hospital, Sydneham of Baltimore, Maryland and Willard Parker in New York City, Haynes Memorial outside of Boston, Municipal Contagious Hospital in Chicago, Illinois and Belmont Hospital in Worcester, Massachusetts. Consequently, we interns never saw contagious diseases in the general hospitals.

Instead of being a depository for patients whose diseases were seen as a threat to the community, these hospitals became centers where infectious diseases could be treated and doctors could be trained.

We moved to Worcester, Massachusetts on July 1, 1949 to live on the first floor of an apartment building on the hospital grounds. We were high on a hill overlooking Route 5 and the railroad yards of Worcester.

My wife could obtain any food or supplies from the hospital to feed all members of our family and I could eat all my meals at home. I also received $100 a month. We were rich.

The hospital had 50 beds, all on one floor, all individual glass cubicles. One nurse could see all patients at all times.

The rules of contagion were very strict. All room doors were always tightly closed. You washed your hands before and after you examined each patient. If anything was dropped on the floor, it was gone. Nurse, doctor or any attendant put on a gown and mask to enter each cubicle.

Children and also some adults were admitted to the hospital with many kinds of contagious diseases: whooping cough, scarlet fever, diphtheria, chicken pox, measles, erysipelas, Mumps, croup, pneumonia and tuberculosis. Most admissions were because the disease was either severe or complicated.

WHOOPING COUGH

After I arrived, our first major disease was Whooping Cough. This was a six-week long disease (2 weeks catarrhal, 2 weeks whooping and 2 weeks convalescent). The white blood count in Pertussis (Whooping Cough) can be as high as 40,000 with a high percent of lymphocytes which sometimes leads to an incorrect diagnosis of leukemia before the children are admitted. Since we had 12-24 infants and children with Pertussis in the hospital at one time, we had a very noisy floor. The paroxysms of coughing prevented us from giving oral medication so we used rectal suppositories of Chloromycetin. Today erythromycin is the drug of choice. It was a no fun disease. Children did not often die from Pertussis but some infants did —usually from secondary pneumonia. We were proud that we had no deaths due to Pertussis during the six months I was at Belmont Hospital.

TYPHOID FEVER

We admitted three patients with typhoid fever. The first patient was acutely ill. The second patient was the sister of the first patient and was not acutely ill. The third patient had been treated at another hospital and had a relapse. Thus we had acute, carrier and relapse stages of typhoid fever. All three responded well to Chloromycetin. Since Chloromycetin was a new drug, I wrote a paper that was published in the New England Journal of Medicine. Parke-Davis, the manufacturer of Chloromycetin, sent a reprint to every doctor in the United States.

POLIOMYELITIS

The fear of polio starts early in the summer and many of our admissions were polio suspects but actually had other diseases. The first child with poliomyelitis arrived on July 21, 1949. Other polio patients followed slowly with the peak week of admissions being September 12-14. Polio is often thought to be a summer disease but in reality it is an August-September disease. From July to December, we admitted 78 patients with poliomyelitis. Three adult men died, ages 23, 26, 29. They had been ill for 10-20 days and continued vigorous physical activity. No child died. Forty-seven patients had no paralysis. Of the paralytic patients, 4 were cervical, 15 were lumbar, 4 were bulbar, 3 were encephalitic and 5 were combined.

We sent spinal fluid to Dr. Cheever's laboratory at Harvard Medical School for polio virus identification and as a source of material to cultivate polio viruses. I visited Boston Children's Hospital for a polio meeting with Dr. John Enders and the orthopedic surgeons and supplied him with spinal fluid from which he grew the polio virus, a pre-step to developing a vaccine.

To avoid transmitting polio to my wife and children, I entered out apartment through the back door, showered and changed my clothes. But one time I was worried that our daughter, Robin, had contracted polio when she developed a high fever. I was relieved when she developed the rash of roseola. She needed some IV fluids and I gave them in her bedroom.

With the nurses and doctors wrestling with polio patients all day, it is amazing that all of us escaped the disease.

When you are young you don't worry about possibilities.

Now that my training years were coming to a close, the next problem was "Where do I practice Pediatrics?" I visited several different cities. Norwood, Massachusetts was a possibility and it was close to Boston. Duluth, Minnesota seemed too remote. South Bend, Indiana seemed likely. The surrounding states, Michigan and Ohio had 300 Pediatricians while Indiana had only 100.

South Bend had a Medical Foundation as fine as any medical center. I could practice good medicine in South Bend. Education for our children looked good. Notre Dame and Lake Michigan were nearby.

26. PEDIATRIC PRACTICE IN SOUTH BEND, INDIANA

We sold or gave away most of our furniture except the bunk beds and crib which could be broken down and packed in the car. We shipped my books by freight. We also shipped our wedding presents from Martha's parents home (where they had been stored) in two barrels.

On December 28, 1949 after spending Christmas with Martha's parents, we drove west on Route 20 in our Chevrolet Malibu with $200.00 in cash. Gary was 4 years of age and Robin was two. I had a job at the South Bend Clinic for $9000.00 the first year. The first thing we did was to establish credit at Sears Roebuck so we could buy a mattress and a vacuum cleaner.

Although I was not expected to start working until 1950, I began making house calls on the last weekend of 1949.

It is amazing how quickly an office becomes full of patients and hospital beds become occupied with children that are your responsibility.

HOUSE CALLS

Each morning I went to the Newborn nursery and Pediatric Ward at Memorial Hospital and then to the same areas at St. Joseph Hospital. The rest of the morning I examined infants and children in my office. During lunchtime I made house calls, picked up some lunch and spent the afternoon seeing more patients in my office. After dinner at home I received and made telephone calls and made house calls. Until they went out of fashion, I made over 1000 house calls each year for 20 years. Sometimes, I also made them late at night or in the wee small hours of the morning.

House calls were a great way to gain valuable information about a family and its resources. When teachers called me about a child's school problems, I often suggested that the teacher visit the home.

Late night calls came when the Studebaker workers arrived home from work. There were 21,000 workers at Studebaker divided into 3 shifts. This is the scenario. After the 3-11 shift, some of the workers would stop at a neighborhood tavern for a few beers. When the worker reached home he would be tired and feeling a little guilty, especially if his wife was angry that he did not come home right after work. The baby would be crying. The following dialogue would occur, "What's the matter with the baby?" "The baby has a fever". "Did you call the doctor? If not I will". He calls the doctor. My phone would ring at 2 AM. Often the problem could be solved over the phone but sometimes I made a house call.

My favorite house call was on one snowy February morning at 2 AM. My door knock was answered by an obviously drunk father. His wife was sprawled exhausted on a chair. The 6-month-old infant was screaming in his crib. His temperature and exam were normal. I changed his diaper; fed him his bottle and he went to sleep. I went home to my bed.

Each home visit was an adventure. First was the problem of the correct address. When my receptionist wrote down the address for the house call she had to make sure the house number was either 819 or 1819, was North or South Main, was the house number displayed and visible from the street.

I learned so much from house calls. I learned not to make home visits during popular TV programs. For my health's sake, I learned it is better to examine the child on the kitchen table or the living room couch instead of in the more contaminated bedroom. If medicine had been prescribed I examined the bottle to be sure that it was the correct medicine and that it had been given. If the medicine had not been given, why? The family might be careless or didn't have the money to buy it. I always carried a supply of sample medicines to use as needed, thanks to the generosity of drug companies. We gave away thousands of dollars worth of medicines.

There was one family to whom I seemed to be making many house calls. I asked if I was the regular doctor for her children. The mother said, "Oh! No. Dr. Murphy is our regular doctor but we don't want to bother her at night."

Another mother who needed frequent home visits would call another doctor for a house call when I did not prescribe an antibiotic. I discovered this fact when the mother phoned both of us to examine her child (who had been in an accident) in the emergency room.

On a rainy summer evening the streets were flooded at vital intersections and I did not believe I could make a requested house call 5 miles away. I suggested to the father that I could phone a prescription to a pharmacy one block from his home and make a house call in the morning. His reply was "Do you expect me to go out on a night like this?"

The father of a family with an impending divorce phoned me from New York City where he had been transferred for work. His wife was still living in South Bend and was scheduled for the final phase of the divorce the next day. He asked if I would talk with her on his behalf because he did not want the divorce. I telephoned his wife and suggested that she ride with me to a house out in the country and we could talk along the way.

At 8 PM we made the house call and she waited in the car. After I had examined the sick child, the child's father walked with me to the car. He said, "I didn't know that your wife was with you. She could have waited in the house." "The only reply I could think of was, "She is not my wife". Fortunately, the couple did not divorce and lived together the rest of their life.

One late winter afternoon a mother requested a house call for her sick child. She said that she had no way to bring the child to my office. When we finished at the office, instead of going home to dinner, I made the house call. I noticed a car in the garage. Inside, the father of the child was happily eating his dinner at the dining room table. I asked the mother why her husband could not have brought the child to my office. She said, "Oh! I couldn't ask him to do that. It's his bowling night."

On another afternoon, a mother asked for an appointment for her very sick child. We told her to please come in right away. She said that she couldn't come until much later. When the mother arrived with her sick child she was so well dressed that my nurse said, "You don't have to dress up when you come in with a sick child". The mother replied, "It was my bridge afternoon".

I was on a house call when our third child, Quincy Adams was born at Memorial Hospital a few days before Christmas. Actually, I was stuck in a snow bank in front of the patient's house. Quincy Adams has sentimental value because that is what I called my Yankee wife when I was courting her in rebel territory in Virginia.

One Christmas Eve I was on call and had to make many phone calls and house calls. I was hoping to finish in time to attend the Christmas Eve Service that ended at midnight at our church. My last house call was a sick child with two bedridden sick parents. Unfortunately, after examining all of them, I arrived at the church just as my wife and children were exiting the church and as the bells proclaimed Christmas Day.

When I made a house call in the winter many of the homes were overheated. One mother in a very warm house asked me why her children were sick all the time. I told her that she kept the house too warm, which encouraged the growth of viruses and bacteria. I did not visit her house again for a long time. When I did, the house temperature was 60 degrees. I asked her if the furnace was working. She said, "Don't you remember? You told me that the house was too warm and since I have turned the temperature down the children have not been ill."

I had two families who were schizophrenic. Making a house call to one family, I noticed the grass was 2-3 feet high, curtains covered all the windows and when I rang the bell, a curtain was parted and a face peered out. Then the door was elaborately unlocked. As I examined the sick child on the living room couch, faces peered out at me from around the corners. When I finished my exam, I announced that the child had tonsillitis. The mother relayed the message to rest of the family behind the other doors.

I could tell the other house a block away. The front gate would be hanging on one hinge; the front yard would be full of toys and would have no grass. Inside, the bathroom sink where I washed my hands, was dirty, the curtains were half hung, and I could tell what the father had eaten for the past two weeks by looking at his trousers. These families were not just sloppy or untidy. They were out of touch with reality. I liked the parents and their children, but I predicted that the children would have great difficulty in becoming part of the real world. Some adjusted in adult life, some did not.

TELEPHONE CALLS

Phone calls are the lifeline of a Pediatric practice but they are also the biggest problem. With our group of pediatricians we had 4 telephone receptionists answering the phones from 8 AM to 6 PM. We received hundreds of calls each day and we had to distinguish between urgent and non-urgent messages.

There are three types of telephone calls that are URGENT. The first is Croup, second is purple rash (for meningococemia) and the third is severe abdominal pain, which can mean appendicitis, intussusception, or volvulus.

To cover the times we were not in the office, we had an Answering Service. All of the persons answering our phones had to be trained to evaluate each call properly. I have great respect for them.

I wonder if anyone realizes the importance of a Pediatrician's wife in answering the telephone. Like our other telephone answering people, she must be kind, supportive and know where her husband is at all times. Even our children got into the act and learned the importance of each phone call.

Beyond the emergencies of croup, purple rashes and severe abdominal pain, there are vomiting, diarrhea and dehydration, diabetic coma, lacerations, head injuries, etc. It is difficult enough for me to sort out what is urgent and what is not and yet we expect our receptionists, nurses and wives to do so. It is particularly difficult when you cover for other doctors and you don't know their patients. You are under pressure not to do something wrong.

I was covering for another doctor when a mother phoned about her 7-day-old infant. Something about her call made me direct her to bring her baby to my office immediately. The baby was being breastfed but his weight had dropped from 7 pounds to 5 pounds. He was dehydrated and malnourished. I rushed him to the hospital. Fortunately he did not need IV fluids because he would drink Pedialyte followed by formula. We corrected the dehydration and he started to gain weight. If I had offered only advice over the phone the infant may not have lived.

I do not prescribe antibiotics over the phone. It is difficult enough to diagnose an illness when I examine a child and I certainly cannot do it over the phone. If a mother said the she could not afford an office call, I saw her child anyway and did not charge.

A family doctor friend of mine prescribed a sulfonamide over the phone when he was called at home. He did not have access to his office records and forgot that the child was allergic to sulfonamide. The child's allergic reaction led to a malpractice law suit.

It could be difficult to convince a mother that her child did not need an antibiotic to get better. A 3 year old child that I was seeing for another doctor had a viral illness. I told the mother that her son would recover without an antibiotic. She said, "But he always gets an antibiotic". I told her that I would phone her the next morning to check on her son. When I did the child had recovered.

27. POLIOMYELITIS

Although I was unaware at the time, my first preparation for work with poliomyelitis began in 1945 as Peripheral Nerve Injury Ward Officer at Cushing General Hospital in Framingham, Massachusetts during World War II. There I examined wounded servicemen and diagnosed the location and extent of their nerve injuries. My next preparation was during my last 6 months in residency training after the war at Belmont Hospital in Worcester, Massachusetts. There I diagnosed many polio cases. We had 78 confirmed Polio admissions but many more Polio suspects. During Polio season many children with fever and headache were evaluated to be sure they did not have Polio. We sent spinal fluid from our polio patients to Dr. John Enders' laboratory at the Harvard School of Public Health in Boston.

NORTHERN INDIANA CHILDREN'S HOSPITAL

After I arrived in South Bend, Indiana on January 1st 1950, Northern Indiana Children's Hospital opened in South Bend in March 1950. NICH had two wings, each with 50 beds, one for acute illness and the other for orthopedic problems. Many of the orthopedic admissions were for the rehabilitation of the children with paralytic polio. The opening of the hospital was well-timed because that summer we had 140 polio admissions and 16 suspects. Eleven children with polio died. Overall there were 303 admissions from March through December in 1950.

In 1951 NICH had 765 admissions with 257 children diagnosed with polio and no deaths. But because of the fear of polio, we admitted 41 who we suspected might have polio.

In 1952 NICH admitted 1431 children of which 250 children had polio with 8 deaths and 66 suspects.

In 1953 NICH admitted 1824 with 85 polio, 2 deaths and 51 suspects.

Children were admitted from 7 Northern Indiana Counties and lower Michigan. (The hospital was only 3 miles from the Indiana-Michigan border.) Across the United States from 1950-1954 there were 28,000 to 58,000 cases of polio each year with between 1450 to 3145 deaths each season.

All of the doctors and nurses at NICH were very aware of the problems of polio. We were immersed in that disease from July to October each year. The nurses and attendants were the brave heroes in their care of the patients.

The acutely ill children with polio were in isolation behind closed glass doors and partitions. The nurses and other medical attendants ministered to the children's needs and communicated between the children and their parents. Many children did not develop paralysis and some of those who did made a complete recovery probably because we used hot packs and other support measures during the acute phase.

Bulbar polio was a problem. Children with this type of polio had difficulty in swallowing their saliva and required frequent suctioning. Sometimes a tracheostomy was needed. Even though the acute phase of bulbar polio was bad, these patients often made a complete recovery.

Children with respiratory difficulty because of chest nerve involvement had to be placed in Emerson Respirators. These "Iron Lungs" were noisy, hot and uncomfortable but they saved lives. Patients in them required almost constant care. I remember one hot August night when the electricity failed during a severe thunderstorm and we had to hand pump 5 respirators for 4 hours.

There were many individual polio stories, some sad, some bad and some amusing.

An 18-year old Italian girl who was engaged to be married was admitted with spinal polio requiring an Emerson respirator. Her fiancée visited daily at first but as the weeks went on he visited less and less and finally not at all.

A teenage girl from LaPorte was admitted with paralysis of one leg but we thought that she was faking. When you really try to lift one leg, you press down with the other leg. We were suspicious that she did not have polio. We asked her to try to lift each leg and she did not press down with the other leg. Her soldier boy friend was coming home from Korea and she had been cheating on him. She thought he would forgive her if she had polio.

We had children who would be admitted in the morning and die before evening in spite of all our efforts. At those times we felt helpless. Yet other times we admitted critically ill children who made a complete recovery.

It was the best of times and it was the worst of times. It was best of times for the many children who lived and were not paralyzed. It was best of times because the nurses, physical therapists, and attendants who, although afraid of catching polio themselves, were so dedicated to their patients that they worked as long as any patient needed care even though it was past their shift.

It was the worst of times because we watched hundreds of patients arrive with polio and knew that some would die or be forever crippled with the disease. We desperately wanted a miracle to prevent polio.

THE NATIONAL FOUNDATION FOR INFANTILE PARALYSIS

The National Foundation for Infantile Paralysis began its support of scientific research in 1938. The first big break came in 1949 when John Enders, Thomas Weller and Frederick Robbins were able to grow the polio viruses on non-nervous tissue. In 1952 David Bodian at John Hopkins and Dorothy Horstmann at Yale demonstrated that polio virus appeared in the blood before passing on to the central nervous system.

Dr. Jonas Salk began his work on the Polio Vaccine in 1951. He first gave the vaccine to children at the D. T. Watson Home for Crippled Children in 1953. These were children who had suffered polio and should not become ill from the vaccine.

Dr. Salk gave a talk to the New Orleans Medical Assembly on March 11, 1954. He said, "For almost two years we have been attempting to devise a practical means for immunizing man against paralytic poliomyelitis. By use of a suitably prepared non-infectious virus vaccine, antibody can be induced readily in amounts equal to that resulting from natural infection. The question that will then be answered by studies under natural circumstances will be: Does a procedure that induces antibody of a certain level in a high proportion of vaccinated persons have a corresponding effect in the prevention of paralytic disease?"

POLIO FIELD TRIAL

A National Advisory Council was formed to determine when and if a full scale field trial could occur to study the effectiveness of a polio vaccine. Almost all of the problems of a trial seemed under control and the Council selected the early spring of 1954 as the appropriate time.

St. Joseph County was chosen one of eight areas in Indiana. Usually the County Health Officer was in charge of the Field Trial but Dr. Nicholas Carter, the Health Officer, asked me to substitute for him.

An advisory committee was in perpetual meeting in Washington, DC to be sure that a safe vaccine was available on time.

The polio viruses for the Field Trial were being grown at the Connaught Laboratories at the University of Toronto. Then the viruses were shipped to Dr. Salk's Lab or to five other commercial laboratories: Parke Davis, Pitman-Moore, Eli Lilly, Wyeth and Cutter where they were made into vaccine.

Each batch of vaccine was tested by the manufacturer, Dr. Salk's Lab and the National Institute of Health Lab. The virus was grown in tissue culture flasks with minced kidney tissues and a nutrient fluid. Each batch of vaccine had elaborate safety and sterility tests.

The virus was injected into a battery of test tubes to be sure that there was no bacterial contamination. Guinea pigs and rabbits were injected to test for contaminating agents in the virus.

The virus was killed by adding formaldehyde. Daily samples were taken to be sure that the virus was killed. Each of the three types of polio virus was then combined for the first time. Then sodium bisulphate was used to neutralize the formaldehyde.

Sterility was tested by injecting the vaccine into bacteriological culture tubes. Safety was tested by injecting 18 monkeys who were watched for 28 days. At the end of this time tissue samples were taken from their spinal cord and brain stem for microscopic examination.

All of this elaborate and time-consuming testing was done to insure the safety and potency of the vaccine which would be used in the field trials.

Walter Winchell had several radio broadcasts and newspaper columns questioning the safety of the vaccine. This bad publicity and other problems delayed the start of the field trials. Because polio was beginning to appear in several Southern counties, they were deleted from the Field Trial.

The steering committee of our County group in charge of the Field Trial began meeting two months before the expected first immunization day. We were fortunate in our choice of two key people: Mrs. James Cloetingh, chairman of volunteers and Mrs. Dan (Gwen) Stiver, chairman of nurses.

The number of physicians, nurses, teachers, school principals, children and other volunteers involved in our county program stretched into the thousands.

In addition to people, we had to have supplies: needles, syringes, alcohol, cotton, tourniquets, blood sampling tubes, record forms, permission slips, reminder cards, thank you notes, film strips, arm bands for volunteers, messages to parents, polio pioneer buttons and polio vaccine.

We also had to have places to give the vaccine. We used public and parochial schools in South Bend, Mishawaka and St. Joseph County. There were 130 different sites.

Due to the excellent Operational Manual supplied by the National Foundation for Infantile Paralysis and the cooperation of hundreds of volunteers, we were ready when the vaccine became available.

Finally on April 25, 1954 I received the following telegram:

"POLIO FOUNDATION UPON RECOMMENDATION OF ITS ADVISORY COMMITTEE HAS RELEASED POLIO VACCINE FOR USE PROVIDED NO REPORTED CASES OF POLIO IN COUNTIES TO BE TESTED WITHIN FOURTEEN DAYS OF START OF PROGRAM. OUR RECORDS INDICATE NO CASES IN YOUR COUNTY SINCE MARCH. EXPECT TO HAVE VACCINE IN YOUR HANDS NOT LATER THAN WEDNESDAY EVENING APRIL 28 POSSIBLY EARLIER"
L.E.BURNEY, MD STATE HEALTH COMMISSIONER

On April 30, 1954 we gave the vaccine to 3,425 second graders and used 13,451 first and third graders as controls. The second injections were given on May 7, 1954 and the third injections were given on June 4.

1954. There were no major reactions or problems associated with the injections of the polio vaccine. My son, Garwood, was one of the second graders to receive the injections.

The feeling of relief and responsibility in conducting a successful field trial of a new polio vaccine can never be minimized. At any point I could have refused to proceed with the injections. If any significant number of children had bad reactions or had developed poliomyelitis, the entire program would have been a disaster.

In 1955, the year after the field trial, 400,000 children were given polio vaccine prepared at the Cutter Laboratory. In preparing the batch of vaccine, the formaldehyde was not mixed properly to kill the polio virus and 204 children developed polio; 153 of the 204 children were paralyzed and 11 died.

If we had been unfortunate enough to have received a batch of this vaccine in our program, none of us doctors would be practicing medicine today. As Dr. Salk stated, "When you inoculate children with a new polio vaccine, you don't sleep well for the next 6 months."

After the polio injections had been given, the real work began. It was necessary to analyze every child with polio and compare the number of cases in those children who received the vaccine with the controls.

The first step in analysis was the accurate diagnosis of poliomyelitis. This was done by stool and blood samples sent to Dr. Frederick C. Robbins in Cleveland, Ohio. If the stool grew polio virus of a certain type and the blood samples showed a rising titre to the same type, then the diagnosis of polio was confirmed.

After the polio season was over, the waiting to learn the results of the field trial began. It took many months to study 650,000 children who had received the vaccine and 1,350,000 who were the controls.

Forty thousand children gave 110,000 samples of blood to determine if the vaccine produced a rise in antibody and thus gave protection against polio.

Over the United States, 20,000 doctors, 40,000 nurses, 14,000 principals, 50,000 teachers and 200,000 lay volunteers using 1,200,000 needles and tons of other supplies were involved in the polio vaccine field trial.

The analysis of the volumes of data was completed by the second week of March 1955. The date to report the findings was Tuesday, April 10, the 10th anniversary of the death of Franklin Delano Roosevelt.

THE POLIO VACCINE IS A SUCCESS
A large group of newspaper and radio reporters crowded into Rackham Hall at the University of Michigan to hear Dr. Thomas Frances report on the Salk vaccine field trial. Edward R. Murrow said, "The sun is warm, the earth coming alive, there is hope and promise in the air. The occasion calls for banners in the breeze and trumpets in the distance."

Dr. Frances stepped to the microphone and said, "The vaccine works. It is safe, effective and potent." The vaccine had proved to be 60-70% effective against Type 1 polio, 90% effective against Type 2 and Type 3.

Against bulbar polio, the vaccine was 94% effective. Dr. Salk then spoke and said he thought that the vaccine could be improved to be 100% effective against all three types of polio virus.

In St. Joseph County in 1954, the year of the field trial, there were 39 cases of polio. In the control groups of the 1st and 3rd grades, there were 10 and 7 cases respectively. In the vaccinated 2nd graders there was only one child with polio and that child was not paralyzed. There were 20 cases of polio in associated family members.

Following the announcement of the effectiveness of the polio vaccine, the immunization of other children began. The National Foundation for Infantile Paralysis had provided funds to stockpile vaccine in hope that the vaccine would be effective.

In St. Joseph County in 1955, the year after the field trial, there were 23 polio cases, 18 in 1956, 5 in 1957 and none since.

A South Bend Tribune article written by Joseph Tierney in October 1957 said: "When they finally get around to erecting monuments for medical victories, one should be put up in St. Joseph County."

Doctors, nurses and volunteers who took part in the polio field trial must be applauded for a job well done. The children, the polio pioneers who participated in the field trial, were the real heroes in the victory over polio.

Those who were too young to remember polio do not realize the change that the vaccine made in America. Of 100 children who developed polio, 50 would have no residual problems, 25 would have mild residual paralysis of an arm or a leg, 15 would be left with severe paralysis and 5 might die. It was the fear of paralysis or death before the advent of the vaccine that made the silent summers so sinister.

In the years before the polio vaccine, the summers were silent. No one gathered at swimming pools, churches or movie theaters. When the polio vaccine removed the fear from the children and their parents, the summers became noisy again.

In the United States there are 250,000 people living today who have had some type of polio. Some of these are now showing muscle weakness, joint problems or other residuals of their previous attack of paralytic polio. Beyond this, there is very little that we remember of the dreaded disease that paralyzed, disabled or killed thousands of children every year for many decades.

In 1967, the St. Joseph County Medical Society asked me to take charge of a Measles Immunization program. Utilizing the same personnel and experience derived from the Polio Vaccine Field Trial, 7827 children received Measles Vaccine at various sites during April 24-28, 1967. Although Measles Vaccine had been available since 1963, the level of participation was poor. This program was an effort to immunize all those children between the ages of 1-14 years who had not been immunized or had not had the disease.

Lack of interest was due to the public belief that measles was not a serious matter. In our publicity about the vaccine, we pointed to the complications of measles: ear infections, pneumonia and encephalitis. Even though the incidence of encephalitis was low, the residuals of severe brain damage were high.

A meeting was held at Rackham Hall in Ann Arbor at the University of Michigan on April 10, 1995 to commemorate the 40th anniversary of the report of the Polio Vaccine Field Trail. My son, Gary, had obtained an invitation for me and I was sitting in the 3rd row while Dr. Jonas Salk spoke about his current virus research.

Although I had corresponded with Dr. Salk in 1954 during the Field Trial, I had never met him. While he made a ceremonial walk around the University campus, I talked with him and thanked him for what he had done for the children of South Bend and the world. I felt honored to have met the physician who had done more for children than any other doctor of the past 50 years. Two months later, in June 1995, Dr. Salk died.

DOROTHY MITCHELL

Dorothy Mitchell had been one of three nurses who were capable of running the entire 50-bed wing of the Northern Indiana Children's Hospital during the polio epidemics. After the Salk vaccine had abolished poliomyelitis, she became my office nurse for 25 years.

She was barely five feet tall. All the children trusted her completely even though they grew taller than she was. She made my job easier by telling me when a child was very sick and she could diagnose a specific illness quicker than I could.

She wore her nursing cap and pin and uniform proudly at all times. She was always clean and proper but she was not afraid to get her uniform dirty. The mothers and the children respected and loved her. She was addressed as "Miss Mitchell" or "Nurse Mitchell."

Her work was her whole life. She was never late in the morning and she would never leave at night until the last patient had been treated. In the winter months when we were seeing 100 plus patients each day, her "day" might end at 8 or 9 PM.

She was one of the last of the hospital trained 3-year Nursing School graduates who were taught that the care of the patient was caring for the patient. When she finally had to stop working because of her health, I am certain it was a very sad day for her, the children and their parents. I know it was for me.

28. REPLACEMENT TRANSFUSIONS

When I first went into private practice, replacement transfusions had just been introduced as the treatment for hemolytic disease of the newborn. If the mother lacked a major blood group factor that the father had, antibodies against that factor would build up in the mother's blood and destroy the baby's blood. RH was the major blood group factor causing a problem. A-B-O, Kell, Duffy and Kidd could also cause hemolytic disease of the newborn. Before our present knowledge of blood groups, a Kidd negative anemic pregnant woman in a hospital was given a transfusion with Kidd positive blood. She died and her newborn infant developed kernicterus and died 5 days later.

A rise in the bilirubin level indicates that the infant's blood is being destroyed which causes brain damage and may even cause death. The purpose of the transfusion is to keep the bilirubin level below 20 mgs%. Usually only one replacement transfusion is sufficient but sometimes a second and rarely a third is indicated.

I learned to do replacement transfusions under Victor Vaughn in 1948, did one in Maine in 1949 and began doing them in Indiana in 1950. We learned that we could do replacement transfusions on premature infants who were having respiratory distress and for some reason their breathing improved dramatically after the transfusion.

We could safely do our replacement transfusions for many years because of the superb quality of the blood testing and cross-matching skills of the technicians at the South Bend Medical Foundation. We had to make the decisions when and how to perform a replacement transfusion but we had complete confidence that the blood supplied by the Medical Foundation Blood Bank was the right blood. Out of a total of approximately 200 replacement transfusions, we lost only one newborn.

A Mother's Love

Canyon Inn
McCormick's Creek Canyon State Park
Spencer, Indiana
December 9, 1954

For Alan to read after he is 18

My dearest Alan,

You have just this morning reached the age of nine weeks, and while a letter would not interest you at all today, sometime you might like to know a little about your start in life, so this is a love letter to tell you about it.

Before you were born we had discovered that my blood was Rh negative and your father's was Rh positive, a combination that might mean trouble for you. Tests of my blood in August and in September before your birth showed that I was building up antibodies to destroy your red blood cells (1 to 64 was the count) but not in sufficient numbers to endanger you before birth. You arrived at 3:07 the morning of Thursday, October 7, a lusty six pound boy and blood tests were immediately begun on you. One hour after your birth your red blood cells were less than half as numerous as they should have been (2,200,000 per cubic mm instead of 5,500,000 normal) and if their destruction continued at that rate, you would have died in another hour. Dr. Erickson immediately gave you a complete blood transfusion via your navel, removing your blood 10 centimeters at a time and replacing it with Rh negative blood. Tests were continued, and it was soon evident that antibodies were still clinging to your body tissues and destroying your blood—you had a second complete transfusion at six o'clock that night.

Very, very fortunately for you and for us. Dr. Erickson had been in Chicago just the previous weekend conferring with two Boston doctors who know more about this blood complication and erythroblastic babies (which you were) than anyone else—he had also written his own doctor's thesis on this subject—but even with these advantages, you presented a problem that he had never encountered before and you were in very grave danger of death. Your skin was yellow-gray; you were in an incubator and had oxygen, drugs, and frequent blood checks through the next few desperately anxious days and nights while your father and I prayed that you would live and that your brain would escape damage, the dreadful threat that accompanies this erythroblastosis. Dr. Erickson told us that if you lived seven days you would probably survive, and never have we counted hour by hour so feverishly.

The fateful bilirubin count was a matter of daily concern—we had been told that brain damage was probable when that count went above 20, and one day yours was 35. Dr. Erickson kept a chart of that count at his own bedside table and watched you devotedly. Twice he telephoned the Boston doctors he regarded so highly; against their advice he gave you a third complete transfusion with its own dangers of infection to bring down the bilirubin count. It was successful—the count dropped to 18—your first perilous seven days had been survived—and on the eighth day I went home from the hospital with your father, leaving you behind in your tiny incubator and feeling very bereft without you—I had been able to peek at you through glass windows at all hours of day and night before, and twice Dr. Erickson had carried you to my hospital room for me to hold very briefly—he showed me the blotches on your back and ears and toes where blood vessels had broken in the throes of your illness and you seemed incredibly weak and tiny.

The day after I left the hospital, Dr. Erickson telephoned me to come to get you—you had thrush, a contagious mouth infection, and could no longer be kept in the hospital nursery. So we brought you home straight from the incubator, so afraid our care would be inadequate—your color still very yellow, your body very thin and wrinkled. No one but your father and I could come into your yellow nursery—our choice of color scheme turned out to be ironic—and your eager brother and sister longed in vain to see you at close range and hold you.

After that, a technician came to your room to give you further Vanden Berg tests for bilirubin count, and finally it dropped to 7—a glorious day for us all. You kept gaining and growing until at 4 weeks Dr. Erickson said you appeared to be quite like any normal baby—and we gave a party for the doctors and their wives to celebrate the happiest of birthdays—your first month birthday.

Now that you are two months old the memories of that most anxious time are already being crowded out, as they should be, by your healthy current demands and the life of the whole family. Daddy and I have felt safe in leaving you for a few days to find some rest and change of scene ourselves. Yet such a short time ago Daddy and your Grandpa White were having nightly telephone conversations about your progress, so many friends were deeply concerned for you and your father and I had to face together the prospect that we would never be able to bring you home to that yellow nursery.

So you can understand, dear little Alan, that we have a very special tenderness for you and a great gratitude to God that you have lived. Your first great battle is won and has given us courage for those to come—I hope the knowledge of it will help you in future battles too. With a heart full of love for you,

Mother

29. CASES

ABDOMINAL PAIN

Appendicitis is the disease of the 10 year old. It is rare in a younger child. I had a 2 year old child in the hospital with salmonella infection causing diarrhea and dehydration. All family members were sick with the same disease. She developed appendicitis and her appendix ruptured before I made the diagnosis. She recovered following surgery and antibiotics but I felt I should have made the diagnosis before the appendix ruptured. Several months later I did make the diagnosis of appendicitis on a 3-year-old girl before her appendix ruptured. Because appendicitis is so rare before the age of ten, it is often overlooked.

The history of appendicitis is very specific. There is first epigastric pain followed by nausea and/or vomiting. The pain then shifts to the right lower quadrant of the abdomen.

Most abdominal pain in children is not appendicitis but appendicitis should be thought of first when there is pain in the right lower quadrant in a child around the age of ten years.

A 17 year old boy developed a sudden right lower quadrant pain about 5 PM on a Friday at work. He phoned his mother who brought him to the ER. The ER physician did not notify me until midnight stating that a diagnosis of appendicitis had been made based on the history, observation and white blood count. The mother chose Dr. W. a competent surgeon, to do the appendectomy.

I phoned Dr. W., apologized for not having examined the child myself, and relayed the mother's request. An appendectomy was done around midnight and Dr. W. left town for the weekend. I examined the young man the next morning and all seemed to be in order. However, as the day went on, he began to vomit and had severe abdominal pain. On Sunday he continued to be ill and I continued to be concerned. The covering surgeon was naturally reluctant to re-operate so it was not until Monday that the original surgeon did. At surgery, the patient was found to have a Spigellian hernia which is a herniation of a portion of the small intestine into the apponeurosis of the Rectus Abdominalis Muscle. Three feet of ileum had become gangrenous and had to be removed.

After 10 days in the hospital the patient went home in good condition. The ER physician was at fault for not taking a proper history. I was at fault for not examining the patient myself in the ER. Diagnosis can be so simple if we listen to the patient. Appendicitis does not start with right quadrant pain.

Robert was an 8 year old boy with abdominal pain. He had been in my office and the ER 36 times. One morning at 6 AM his mother called me at home. She said, "Robert has pain again". I examined Robert in my office at 7 AM. He was in obvious severe pain with visible loops of hyperperistalsis present. This meant that he had intestinal obstruction and needed immediate surgery. By 8 AM I assisted Dr. George Plain in removing 6 feet of small bowel, which had been trapped in an internal hernia. This is an unusual hernia where the intestine slips through an opening where the duodenum is retroperitoneal. On previous occasions the intestine had evidently managed to escape from entrapment spontaneously but not this time.

A common cause of abdominal pain is fecal impaction. The child is constipated and has great difficulty in having a bowel movement. He may soil his underwear. He may even have diarrhea because a loose bowel movement can occur around the packed feces. As the child tries to have a bowel movement, it hurts so he suppresses the urge.

This suppression continues for many days and finally the child's rectum is so packed with feces that it is impossible for the bowels to move. He stains his underwear and may develop a bad odor. It is amazing how long a child with problem goes undetected by his parents or undiagnosed by his doctor. I wonder how many children there are with undiagnosed fecal impactions. How easy it is to do a manual rectal exam. Changing bowels habits means working with the child and parents and it takes time.

A mother from Leiter's Ford, Indiana came with her 5-year-old son to see me because he would not eat or gain weight. His exam was normal except for fecal impaction. His parents followed my directions to remove the impaction and then to prevent its recurrence. He returned to my office weekly for follow up and education. Three months later, he had grown 2 inches and gained 10 pounds.

There is another likely cause for a strange odor. This odor is caused by a foreign body retained in the body usually in the nose. The child has placed a piece of Kleenex, a pea, or almost anything in one side of his nose. He will have a one sided nasal discharge. Removal of the object usually solves the discharge and the odor. A discussion with the child is in order. We discourage children from placing objects in any body opening.

DIABETES

Often an interest in a specific disease begins when the doctor has a patient with that disease. One of my first interests was infants born to diabetic mothers. When I first began practice, I found that newborns of pregnant diabetic mothers had major problems because the mothers were not well controlled. Priscilla White, MD of the Joslin Clinic established guidelines to control the blood sugars of the mothers and to handle their newborn.

Blood sugar in the newborn may be low due to the mother's insulin and the infant may develop respiratory distress. The infant's calcium may drop after the first few days and the bilirubin may rise. We anticipated and corrected these abnormalities as necessary and the newborns did well.

Many years ago one of my young diabetic mothers did not follow directions. She had moved to a rural community with a small hospital. I recommended that she go to a larger hospital where obstetricians and pediatricians familiar with infants of diabetic mothers were available. She did not heed my advice and delivered in the small hospital. Unfortunately, the infant died.

When she became pregnant again, she went to the same small hospital. The newborn was transferred to a regional center but too late to save the baby.

She moved closer to South Bend. When she was pregnant for the third time, I begged her to go to Memorial Hospital where we had an intensive care nursery. Several months later at 6 AM a nurse from the nursery of a small hospital nearby called me to tell me that this mother had delivered and that the infant had a blood sugar of zero. I called the intensive nursery at Memorial Hospital and asked them to send a transport ambulance to pick up the infant at the small hospital.

In the meantime, I went to the small hospital and examined the infant who acted normal in spite of the zero blood sugar. I told the mother that we would like to send her baby to Memorial Intensive Care Newborn Nursery. The mother objected. "My husband won't let you transfer my baby. The last time we did that the baby died." In spite of the mother's objections, we transferred the baby anyway. After giving the infant IV glucose, some oxygen and calcium and putting the infant under a bililight for a few days, the infant was discharged home.

What a difference an adequate intensive care nursery with experienced well trained nurses made in the life of a newborn infant of a diabetic mother.

In recent years as control has improved in the care of diabetic mothers, the problems of the newborn have lessened.

My youngest diabetic patient was a six-month-old infant referred with vomiting and dehydration. As I was examining the infant, he urinated and an alert pediatric nurse said, "He has diabetes". Her diagnosis was correct. Insulin and IV fluids quickly improved a very sick infant. We wondered how difficult it would be for the infant to be on a diet and insulin regulation. He was very cooperative. He drank and ate everything we gave him and we regulated his blood sugars easily on 2 units of insulin a day.

A child may develop diabetes suddenly with loss of weight and dehydration without alarming the parents. Each year several children with new diabetes were admitted to the hospital in a coma.

Low blood sugar can occur in a child when he has his insulin shot in the morning and rushes off to school without breakfast. One 12-year-old girl who did this had a convulsion in school at 10 AM. The school nurse thought that the child had epilepsy instead of realizing that her seizure was due to hypoglycemia.

A family traveling through town brought their 5 year old girl to the hospital emergency room with abdominal pain. She had Mumps with pancreatitis. Her urinalysis revealed that she also had diabetes. Viral illnesses can attack and injure the beta cells of the pancreas.

Children who have diabetes usually are cooperative and easy to regulate. Adolescents on the other hand can be very difficult. They do not want to be different than their friends. They do not like the strict diet, testing their blood sugars, and giving themselves insulin injections.

They become sloppy in their diabetic control without immediate consequences. We tried to teach them that good control now meant a long life without eye, kidney or liver problems later.

Newer forms of insulin, self-testing blood sugar kits, tests such as Hemoglobin A1c, insulin pumps, and better patient education have greatly improved the care of the diabetic patients and allowed them to live longer with fewer complications.

RHEUMATIC FEVER

Emily was a 14 year old girl sent to the hospital by her Plymouth doctor. It was quickly apparent that Emily had acute rheumatic fever. I asked a cardiologist to see her to help make the decision between aspirin or cortisone for her treatment. We agreed on aspirin and bed rest while we watched her carefully each day.

Emily was not very sick during the first 5 days but then became very short of breath. Her chest x-ray was normal on admission but now had patches of fluffy infiltrates. This could mean either rheumatic pneumonia or overwhelming sepsis. I asked Dr. Gary Fromm, a pulmonologist, to see Emily. We agreed that we needed a lung biopsy to guide her therapy. Jim Kelly, a cardiac surgeon removed a piece of her right lower lobe for biopsy and also placed a Swan-Ganz catheter to measure her central venous pressure.

The slides were immediately examined by the pathologist who confirmed the diagnosis of rheumatic pneumonia. Although I had treated many children with rheumatic fever many years before, I had never seen rheumatic pneumonia. The current pediatric textbooks state that the complication is 100% fatal. We met with the parents and other relatives in a small conference room. We told them what we had found and that Emily's prognosis was not good. The other doctors left the room and I stayed to talk with the parents. I said that Dr. Cresser, the anesthesiologist told me that Emily fought so hard when he tried to intubate her that he was afraid he couldn't do it. I thought that anyone with that much spunk was going to live and I told the parents so.

We started Emily on massive doses of steroids and put her on a respirator. She improved daily. After 2-3 days she could breathe on her own and we gradually reduced the steroids. In two more weeks, she was strong enough to continue care at home. In two months she became a normal teenager. Emily finished high school, was graduated from college, married and I danced with her at her wedding.

30. RASHES

Many times mothers phoned about their child's rash. My standard answer was "I can not diagnose a rash over the phone.". What I visualized over the phone was not what I saw in the office.

Diseases with a rash have always intrigued me. Although a rash can be confusing, there are clues that help make the diagnosis.

One of the first diseases with a specific rash that I learned about was Fifth Disease, also known as Erythema Infectiosum. I was intrigued not so much for the rash as for the name. Why is it called Fifth Disease? Is there a First, Second, Third, and Fourth Disease? Erythema Infectiosum was originally called Fifth Disease because it was the fifth one discovered in a series of childhood exanthems all caused by different viruses. First there was Measles (Rubeola), Second was Scarlet Fever, Third was German Measles (Rubella), Fourth was Dukes' Disease, Fifth was Erythema Infectiosum and Sixth was Roseola (Exanthem Subitum).

Fifth Disease is caused by parvovirus B19. The rash begins on the face giving a slapped cheek appearance and spreads to the trunk and extremities and lasts about a week. Exercise, bathing and exposure to sunlight intensify the rash. Scarlet Fever, Rubella, ECHO, Roseola, Mononucleosis, and Cosackie viruses are confused with Fifth Disease but the slapped cheek rash is the key to the diagnosis

Every mother knows Roseola. This disease occurs in infants during the first three years. The patient has a high fever, usually 101'-104', physical exam is normal, but after a few days the fever returns to normal and a generalized macular rash appears.

However, during the fever period, the mother and doctor worry that the infant has a disease that should be treated. In Roseola the white blood count is low which may give some indication that treatment is not necessary. The infant should be watched closely until the rash appears.

With the increasing use of immunizations, many childhood diseases have become uncommon and doctors may never see a patient with these specific rashes.

31. CONVULSIONS

Convulsions were a common problem. High fever was thought to be the cause of some convulsions. We now feel that the toxic onset of an illness may be the cause rather than the fever.

During 1950-1970 I almost always had an infant or a child in the hospital with meningitis. Because we worry about meningitis in a child with seizures we often feel compelled to do a lumbar puncture. Spinal taps are dreaded by parents, but done by a competent pediatrician can be a simple procedure. The cause of meningitis most often was H. influenza bacillus with pneumococcus and meningococcus being less common. But now with the development of a vaccine against H.influenza infections, the cases of meningitis have decreased dramatically.

Truman was a 10 year old Amish boy sent from Shipshawanna to Northern Indiana Children's Hospital in 1953. He had tuberculous meningitis, which was almost 100% fatal. We started him on streptomycin, isoniazid and paraminobenzoic acid. ACTH (Adrenocortical thyrotrophic hormone) had just been developed. We reasoned that ACTH might reduce the inflammation of the meninges and allow our other medicines to pass through into the brain. No one knew the correct dose but we decided on 40 mgms IM daily. We watched Truman for any side or toxic effects of the ACTH. Aside from becoming a little puffy and developing a great appetite, Truman improved. After 6 weeks, his spinal fluid became normal and we sent him home on continued care. He made a complete recovery.

Almost 25 years later a 5 year old black boy was admitted to St. Joseph Hospital with meningitis. Although he had a negative tuberculin test and a normal chest x-ray, I knew that he had tuberculous meningitis and began treatment. This time we used prednisone orally instead of ACTH. To prove the diagnosis of tuberculosis meningitis it is necessary to inject guinea pigs with spinal fluid from the patient. It takes six weeks before we can examine the liver and spleen of the guinea pigs to confirm the diagnosis. While we were continuing treatment and awaiting results with the guinea pigs, the boy became blind and deaf due to increased intracranial pressure. A ventriculoperitoneal shunt relieved the CNS pressure. His eyesight and hearing returned to normal and he was discharged after 6 weeks for further treatment at home. His family moved away but I had the great pleasure of seeing him 10 years later. He visited me as a healthy 15 year old to thank me for treating him 10 years ago. His eyesight and hearing were normal and he was looking forward to entering college.

How could anyone not want to be a Pediatrician?

Some children with seizures have epilepsy. The type of seizure can be determined by an EEG and controlled by various medicines. Years ago we only had phenobarbital and dilantin but now we have many anticonvulsants which control 90% of seizures. For those children whose seizures aren't controlled by medicine, surgical excision of the specific areas of the brain may stop the convulsions.

Seizures can be frightening to the parents and the child. Usually a seizure is not life threatening. Jennifer, a 5 year old girl, was an exception. Twice she had to be hospitalized with status epilepticus, which means we could not control her seizuring. We sent her to Cleveland Clinic where they did brain surgery and it controlled her seizures. After all the scary stuff Jennifer went through, she said to me "Dr. Erickson. You are my best friend."

How many of you have a 5 year old girl as your best friend?

ATTENTION DEFICIT HYPERACTIVITY DISORDER

One of the more common problems of children in the past 50 years has been Attention Deficit Hyperactive Disorder. ADHD has been diagnosed and misdiagnosed in thousands of children by family doctors, psychologists, psychiatrists and teachers. This diagnosis must be considered in any child who is not doing well in school. Organic diseases such as hyperthyroidism must be ruled out. Medicines such as Phenobarbital which can cause hyperactivity must be stopped. Visiting their home is a way to evaluate conditions in the home. Is there an alcoholic father or mother or relative in the home? Are the parents psychotic? Is the TV set on 24 hours a day?

Teachers are the best observers in referring children for evaluation for ADHD. Some children have a reading problem, some do not. Do they pay attention? Do they sit still in school? Are they vocally hyperactive or physically hyperactive or a combination of both? Usually a boy is more likely to have ADHD than a girl.

Children with ADHD can be difficult to manage because many do not like to have any restrictions placed on their behavior. These children are not neurotic or psychotic and we must be careful when evaluating or treating them not to destroy their self-esteem. Behavior modification is useful up to a point but most ADHD children need some specific medicine. Ritalin was usually my choice.

The most important point in helping children with hyperactivity is to make the proper diagnosis. Discussions and cooperation with the parents and the teachers is essential. Everyone must be on the same page in knowing the facts about ADHD in relation to each individual child. I have found the best source of information for parents and teachers is an article, "Managing Stimulant Medication for Attention/Deficit/ Hyperactivity Disorder" by Esther H. Wender, MD which appeared in the June 2001 issue of Pediatrics in Review.

SCHOOL PHOBIA

A usually preventable problem is school phobia. Phobia means fear but the problem is not fear of school. The fear is of leaving home.

The stage can be set when a mother tearfully brings her child to kindergarten. An experienced teacher knows how to help the mother and her child make the transition from home to school. The child feels more secure knowing that his or her mother is at home waiting for the child's return so they can tell her all about their school day. The situation is not helped by the working mother who is not at home so it is a good policy for the mother to arrange her working hours so she can be at home at that crucial time. The mother should always give her work and home phone number to her child and the teacher so that she can be reached in an emergency.

When I suggested to one of my non-working mothers that she be home when her son returned from school, she said, "If you think I'm going to give up my bridge club to do that, you are wrong." Her son had many emotional difficulties during his school years and later in life. Another mother said haughtily that her children were self-sufficient and could take care of themselves until she arrived home.

Parents can cooperate with the teacher to prevent school phobia but if they can't then they should seek out a pediatrician skilled in treating school phobias.

Knowing the family dynamics and relationship is important. A 7 year old girl whose mother was pregnant refused to go to school. The girl had been watching an afternoon soap opera at a neighbor's house. The mother in the TV program died when she had a baby and the 7 year old worried the same thing would happen to her own mother.

A mother and father in another family argued in front of the children. The mother said to her husband, "Someday I may not be here when you come home from work." Hearing this, her daughter refused to go to school. She was afraid her mother might carry out her threat.

A child with school phobia does not say, "I don't want to go to school. The child says, "I have a headache" or "I have a tummy ache." To rule out organic disease, it is necessary for the pediatrician to take a good history and do a physical examination and if necessary lab tests and x-rays. If no disease is found, then the pediatrician can give the child careful reassurance that it is OK to go to school. Then the parent takes the child to school, after alerting the teacher and the relatives. The longer the child remains out of school, the more difficult the return will be. After convincing the mother and the relatives that the child has no physical illness, but the child still does not want to attend school, the pediatrician must discover the real reason. This may take some time.

Sometimes that is not easy as was the case of a very intelligent 10 year old girl. She agreed to go to school. After the mother drove her daughter to school and jumped out of the car to help her child into the school, the child locked all the doors in the car and refused to unlock them.

32. KINDERGARTEN DROPOUTS

I always took great delight in rescuing children from wrong diagnoses. Two children had been rejected by kindergarten. The first child was a 6 year old girl who was diagnosed as being too hyperactive to sit still in kindergarten. This immediately caught my attention because most little girls can sit very still. I learned that she was taking phenobarbital for convulsions. Often, Phenobarbital can make a child hyperactive. After I investigated further, I determined that this little girl did not need the phenobarbital. As soon as we stopped the phenobarbital, the hyperactivity disappeared and she returned to kindergarten.

The other child was a 6 year old boy who is the subject of my favorite rejection story. On his first day of kindergarten, his teacher noted that he appeared to be shy and lacking in social skills. She referred him to the school psychologist who concluded, after testing, that the boy was severely mentally retarded and did not belong in public school.

The parents came to my office in great distress to tell me what had happened. I had him tested by a private psychologist whose testing showed the boy was not retarded and was in fact very intelligent.

The problem was that the parents worked and left their son with their next-door neighbor. The parents came home from work late and tired, fed the child and put him to bed. Neither the neighbor nor the parents provided intellectual or social stimulation. With great difficulty, I convinced the school to accept the boy into kindergarten and then discussed better parenting with the parents. When the boy was in high school, he won first prize in math for the State of Indiana.

33. THE DARK SIDE OF PEDIATRICS

One of the best rewards of being a Pediatrician is that few infants and children die during the years they are under our care. The result is that when a child does die, we don't know how to deal with the death. If a child died, I never went to his funeral. The death of a child was very traumatic for me and I always felt that I had failed my responsibility. Fortunately, another child would need my attention and passage of time would relieve my depression.

In my early years of practice before we knew very much about respiratory distress in the newborn, one of my newborns died. I was so devastated that the mother of the baby was consoling me. She said, "I am Catholic. I'll be pregnant again within a year and I'll have you take care of my next baby." She was and I did.

Early one Christmas morning, I went to the hospital to examine a five-year-old girl whom I had admitted two days before with viral encephalitis. The prognosis with this disease is usually very good. For some reason, her condition suddenly worsened and she died.

This is the no-fun part of being a doctor: to try to explain to the child's parents why their daughter died and to help them with their grief while you are lamenting your own inadequacies. Then you go home to your own children and present a happy exterior while you are weeping inside – and to do this on Christmas morning.

ACCIDENTS

Many deaths in children are due to accidents. Choking and falling are the leading causes in infants while auto accidents have become the main cause of death in children and adolescents. The children may be drivers, passengers or pedestrians.

Ruptured spleens were occasional events usually the result of automobile accidents. During 1950-1960 surgical removal of the bleeding spleen was the treatment of choice. During later years it was considered best not to remove the spleen unless absolutely necessary.

Shirley, a 17 year old young woman rode her motorcycle over a railroad track and fell on one of the railroad ties. She had an obviously damaged spleen. Under the new guidelines the surgeon and I watched her in the hospital for 7 days. Since she was stable, we sent her home with instructions. The morning after discharge, her father called frantically to say that he found Shirley lying unconscious on her bedroom floor. We instructed him to bring her back to the hospital immediately. The surgeon and I went to the Emergency Room to await her arrival. We waited a long anxious hour before the ambulance arrived with Shirley. The explanation: "We had to fix a flat tire." We started a blood transfusion and brought Shirley to the operating room where the bleeding spleen was removed. Shirley recovered and sold her motorcycle.

So much for the policy of watchful waiting for spleen injuries.

Some of the worst childhood accidents that I have treated have been due to motorcycles and I warn my patients about them. Peter, an 18 year old young man, limped into my office. He laid his motorcycle helmet on my desk. The helmet was so gorgeous I was tempted to try it on but I resisted. "As you know", he said, "It was very difficult to persuade my parents to let me buy a motorcycle. They finally agreed and I've ridden it over 200 miles this weekend. My back is killing me. I have a bad headache and I burned both my legs on the exhaust pipes." "What's the problem?" I asked. His answer, "I never want to ride a motorcycle again and I don't know how to tell my parents".

St. Joseph Hospital emergency Room telephoned me at my office at five o'clock one fall afternoon. A five year old boy had been hit by a car and was in the ER. This was in the time when there were no ER doctors so you treated your own patients. My office is only 2 minutes away. The boy was in an examining room. The nurses were giving him CPR and IV fluids. It was obvious to me after a few minutes that resuscitation would not help. He had been dead on admission.

I came out of the examining room. The boy's parents were sitting there expecting me to tell them that their son was all right. He had been playing at a friend's house. His mother telephoned him to come right home before it became dark. He ran across the street without looking and was hit by a car. I had to tell his parents that there was nothing that we could do – their son was dead.

A 16 year old girl was babysitting. The 18 year old brother of the baby said, "I will drive you home". One block from the house he drove into a telephone pole. The babysitter sustained a contussed lung and kidney and a fractured femur. It took six months of hospital care before she could return home.

On New Year's Eve a young gentleman offered a ride home to a girl who wanted to leave a party early. He drove into a tree. He sustained a head injury. The girl died.

One of my mothers lost her two daughters a year apart in auto accidents due to drunk drivers.

S.I.D.S

One difficult house call was the dread of every pediatrician, going to the home of a family where the baby has died. But I always went. SIDS – Sudden Infant Death Syndrome usually occurs to 6 month old infants.

One Christmas Day I made a SIDS house call. After talking with the parents, I noted the 14 year old baby sitter crying in the corner of the room. I shifted my attention to her and tried to relieve her of any feelings of responsibility for the infant's death.

On another SIDS house call when I entered the home, the living room was filled with friends and relatives all of whose children were patients of mine. Their unspoken question hung in the air: "Why did this baby die?"

This is what I said; "Right now I don't know why Jimmy died. With the parents' permission we will do an autopsy. I want to be sure as the baby's doctor that I did not overlook some condition that I should have treated. The parents want to be sure that they did not overlook anything either. There are many theories as to why infants die in their first year of life. So far no one knows the cause. With the parent's permission we will tell you the results of the autopsy. We also do the autopsy to be sure that Jimmy did not have some disease that might be communicable to you or your children."

No cause of death was found at autopsy. Two years later Jimmy's mother delivered healthy twin boys. We now believe that having infants sleep on their backs may lessen the possibility of SIDS death.

Because of my sister's death and the memory of her funeral, I found it difficult to attend the funeral of another child. I tried to console parents but I did not do it well.

It took many years before I realized that I could not save every child and that the parents of the child needed my help in the grieving process. I visited the parents in their home or attended the funeral. Doing this helped the parent and it helped me.

34. PREVENTION

I am a firm believer that the most important role of a pediatrician is in providing anticipatory guidance that includes pointing out hazards along the way.

When an infant or a child starts talking, parents and other family members should pay attention and listen. Why is this so important?

I believe that stuttering is an almost completely preventable problem if the parents stop what they are doing and listen to the child. If the parents ignore the talking child, the child may try to talk faster to get the parents' attention. The parents should not say, "Slow down" or "Start over". It helps to stoop or sit down to the child's level to communicate more equally.

By approaching the child's early talking in this way, the development of speech problems and stuttering may be prevented.

Another preventable illness is urinary tract infections in girls. Why girls and not boys? Boys have a very long urethra and girls have a short urethra. So when a boy takes a bath, the bacteria in the bath water does not travel up his urethra into his bladder where as it does in girls. The bath water is contaminated with bacteria (E.coli) from the anal area when the child sits in the tub. To prevent UTI in girls is easy. Keep them out of the bathtub. Start them as early in life as possible to take showers.

One of the most gratifying aspects of being a pediatrician is the influence we have in guiding children. It is great to help save a life but we can also motivate, encourage and help them make important decisions. Along with parents, teachers, coaches, clergymen I share the fun of helping children grow up.

Vernell's mother was very disturbed when she came to see me. Vernell was 12 years of age and he became very critical of his mother because he had no father. His mother was a good woman who worked as a nursing assistant at the hospital. I invited Vernell to have lunch with me at the hospital and then we made rounds on my patients. I told Vernell that his mother was a friend of mine and I admired her. Vernell did not change his attitude suddenly but I pushed him in the right direction. He grew up, married, and has two healthy children who have both a mother and a father.

Joseph was a patient from birth. He had a normal childhood, grew up and went to Notre Dame. He was graduated magna cum laude with a degree in civil engineering. He accepted a job offer from the Bendix Corporation in South Bend. Three years after graduation, he told me that although he enjoyed engineering, he really wanted to be a doctor. He knew that he needed certain pre-med courses before he could apply to medical schools so he took them at Notre Dame while still continuing to work at Bendix. He received straight A's in all the pre-med courses and finished them in two years. He applied to medical schools and began the months of waiting. He was rejected everywhere he applied.

He was used to rejection. When he was a senior at Notre Dame he was engaged to be married. The girl's parents did not think Joseph was good enough for her and she called off the wedding.

In early September Joseph phoned me. He said, "Indiana University just called me and said that a girl from Ohio did not show up for admission to the medical school and I could have her place. What should I do?" My answer, "Go for it". Joseph quit his engineering job and went to medical school. He was graduated from Indiana University Medical School four years later. I regretted not being able to attend his graduation but I said to him, "Send an invitation to the parents of the girl who did not think you were good enough for her".

We did attend his marriage to a wonderful nurse in Indianapolis, Indiana. Joseph decided that he wanted to be a pediatrician and finished the 3-year residency program at Riley Children's Hospital in Indianapolis.

35. ADOLESCENTS

ANOREXIA

Notre Dame, St. Mary's College and Culver Military Academy along with the local high schools were sources of a great supply of teenage girls with anorexia nervosa. After an interview about anorexia was published in the South Bend Tribune, we received many phone calls from 20-30 year old women. The older the patient and the older the disease the more difficult it was to treat it successfully. Many of the 20-30 years old patients seemed to need to confess what they had done in the past or were still doing. Many were married but had kept their anorexia or bulimia secret from their husbands. The reason for some of the married women seeking help was because they wanted children but could not become pregnant. Others confessed to binge eating on candy or food without too many serious side effects.

Susan was a 22 year old woman who came to me when she was still single. She did not change her behavior or her eating pattern even though I tried to help her. One day she announced that she was engaged to be married. I thought that this event might be the key to helping her. Little did I know how wrong I was. Susan and her husband went camping on their honeymoon. Food preparation was spotty and sparse and Susan managed to eat very little. When Susan returned home from the honeymoon, she ate her "breakfast" before her husband arose. She ate very little lunch and ate supper before her husband arrived home. I had hoped that Susan and her husband would eat meals together but she managed to outflank me. Marriage did not change Susan's anorexia and I gave up trying.

Alice was a married woman when she came to see me because she wanted to have a baby. In common with others with anorexia she was not menstruating. Alice began eating proper amounts of food and gaining weight but she did not menstruate. Six months after her first visit she was still not menstruating when she came in for a routine exam. I palpated a mass in her lower abdomen. Did I overlook an ovarian tumor? I was disturbed. But an ultra sound showed that the mass was her uterus tipped to one side and that she was pregnant. Alice ate well during her pregnancy because I stressed that she was eating for herself and her baby. She delivered a healthy 7-pound male infant.

My brief months with the adult women who have an eating disorder made me realize there were too many of them and I happily went back to my teenage girls whom I understood much better.

Anorexia begins for one or two reasons: fear of being fat or fear of growing up. The usual mechanism at the beginning of anorexia is that the girl feels fat and she may be. TV is a big factor in making people feel fat. TV presents beautiful people with ideal thin bodies. Dieting is in vogue and diets are remedies for all social and psychosomatic ills. It is "in" to diet.

The girl starts to lose weight. At some point she cannot stop losing weight and continues on a toboggan slide until someone else intervenes. Those who fear growing up think that if they do not eat, they won't develop breasts or menstruate and then they won't have to cope with all the problems of being an adult.

Girls who do not accept their bodies and are afraid to proceed with their maturation, lack self-esteem and do not seem to have separate identity from their mother. Therefore, they cannot form any major relationship outside the family, which is the important task of adolescence. They despair about their bodies and themselves and about life itself. They are often depressed and some may be suicidal.

The feeding role of the mother in the family can be a factor. Food is equated with health and is a symbol of the mother's role and authority. Giving food enhances the mother's status, self-esteem, and security. In the anorexia family, food is the currency of interaction. The mother presses food on her young child insisting that the child eat it. The child is surrounded by plenty and given everything she needs. Actually, her needs are anticipated. Her development is always an achievement of her mother, not of herself. She conforms to her mother's needs and is described as a "good" child. But the mother is intruding upon the child's world and not allowing the child to be appropriately hungry or full. In defense the child may starve herself. Refusing to eat is also the first major act of autonomy.

The anorexic patient defends her position with aggression and apparent certainty. But underneath it all there are feelings of uncertainty and impotence. Anorexia helps make her feel special and unique.

Anything that the mother does will make matters worse. The mother has to learn to do nothing.

The child is caught between guilt at not meeting her mother's need for attachment and the child's own need for withdrawal. When the child overcomes her fear of experiencing her own feelings, she is able to communicate her inner thoughts and contribute positively to her own therapy.

Management of anorexia involves understanding and treatment of an entire family in distress. The anorexia child has an intense interest in food. Instead of confronting the child, we send her to an anorexia-aware dietitian who will teach her proper nutrition. The pediatrician and the dietitian can gently try to find the underlying reasons for the child's anorexia. At the same time we try to help the mother and other relatives understand their role in the child's therapy.

The real pathology in anorexia is not weight loss. It is how the child feels about herself. Honest communication between pediatrician, dietitian, mother and child is the first step. Anorexics may be manipulative and deceitful. Only when the patient trusts her doctor and the dietitian can effective treatment begin.

Helping the child gain trust in her own ability to help herself and build her self esteem is a slow process. To be able to help an anorexic teenager change from a helpless victim to become a healthy active participant in living is very satisfying. Many of my anorexia patients have gone on to become dietitians or doctors. My youngest patient was 11 years of age when she started anorexia but today she is an Emergency Room physician.

One of my patients was a senior in high school when she had an eating disorder. Her weight dropped from 160 to 110 pounds. She was improving slowly until an event accelerated her recovery. As a graduation present, she was given an airplane trip to Boston to visit two maiden aunts. Both of the aunts worked. The first morning the girl was there, she looked around and found very little food in their house. It was the first time that no one urged her to eat. When she came home to Indiana, she told her mother that the aunts had been trying to starve her. From that moment on, she changed her behavior and rapidly gained her normal weight back. Four years later she was graduated from Notre Dame.

Some patients required some time in the hospital at the beginning of their therapy. They were admitted either because their weight loss was sufficient to have caused physical illness or we needed to try to establish better eating habits under supervision. We did not threaten them with tube feedings or IV fluids. The nurses were experienced with anorexia and were kind and supportive and tried to establish an atmosphere of trust. The few children who needed to be in the hospital stayed only 7-10 days.

TEENAGE GIRLS

There is one time when a doctor shouldn't listen to the patient and that is when a teenage girl denies being sexually active. Pregnancy must not be ruled out in any female in the menstruating age group who has a complaint.

Susan was a 16-year-old girl who had moved to Indianapolis. Her mother brought her back to me because she was vomiting and had abdominal pain. Her mother was angry with the Indianapolis doctor because he suggested that Susan might be pregnant. Susan needed IV fluid and was admitted to the hospital where a urinalysis showed a urinary tract infection. She was treated with Bactrim. Susan continued to vomit and was readmitted to the hospital. This time, in spite of Susan's denial of sexual relations, a pregnancy test was done and was positive. Even after the positive test Susan continued to deny.

Don't ask teenagers if they are sexually active and if you do ask don't listen and if you do listen, don't believe.

One of the pregnant couples I saw was a star football player and his cheerleader girl friend. They decided to marry. The only problem was that the boy wanted to wait until the end of the football season. His father learned of the pregnancy and offered his son $10,000 each year for 4 years if his son would go to college instead of marrying the girl. The boy took the offer but he flunked out during his first year of college. The girl had the baby, raised her daughter by herself and so far has never married.

Another teenage girl decided that she would have her baby and give the baby up for adoption. She went to Indianapolis for delivery, saw her baby and changed her mind. She brought the baby home for her mother to raise and took off for college. The girl's parents later divorced largely because of the stress of having a new infant in the home.

One night, my home doorbell rang and there stood two scared teenagers. I knew their problem before they even told me. The girl was pregnant and they wanted to know where to go to have an abortion. Also, they were afraid to tell their parents. I let each of them talk until they were somewhat relaxed. I did not preach. I told them they had three options: abortion, keep the baby, or adoption. We tried to talk logically about each choice. I urged each of them to talk with their parents.

Sometimes, when the girl tells her parents that she is pregnant, the mother will say, "How could you do this to me?" If I talk with the mother of the girl, I try to explain that the girl did this to herself. Now, she needs her mother's support in helping her make a decision. Unfortunately, most mothers reacted emotionally only and compounded the problem.

There is no easy solution for all the problems caused by unmarried teenage pregnancy. Prevention is a complicated process. Parents of teenagers often have difficulty communicating with them. As a pediatrician I try to teach the facts of life but I may be in conflict with parents' wishes, particularly if they are Catholic. I do my best but if a teenager becomes pregnant, I feel that I have failed.

When young lovers marry because the girl is pregnant, the possibility of divorce increases greatly.

A distressed mother said that her 3 year old daughter was very difficult to control. The girl seemed to hate her mother. I learned that the mother had married because she became pregnant. The mother had marriage problems and blamed it on her daughter. When I pointed out to the mother that her daughter was not the cause of her marriage problems the mother understood. Once the girl felt loved and accepted by her mother, not only did their relationship improve but so did the marriage.

Sometimes there are surprising outcomes to a difficult problem. I discovered that a 12 year old girl was pregnant when I did her school exam. I believed that the girl's father would have shot the boy responsible if I had not spent an entire afternoon dissuading him. The girl had the baby. The boy and girl married several years later. They now have 5 children and are one of the happiest couples I know.

36. FAMILY TIES

EVERY CHILD NEEDS TWO PARENTS

It was a simple story by a mother of two teenage boys that made me change from child oriented pediatric practice to family oriented pediatric practice. The mother brought her sons in for a routine exam. She said that her visit had been delayed because her husband died. I encouraged her to tell me the history of his illness. Her husband came home from work each day about 5 PM, took a bottle of beer from the refrigerator, worked around the house while continuing to drink beer until he ate dinner at 10 PM. On weekends he drank a case of beer. He did not drink at work or get drunk. He was a good husband and father. Unfortunately he had a heart attack and died suddenly a few months ago. His wife did not realize there was a problem. I was very disturbed because her husband's excess beer consumption, which had elevated his triglycerides to the level of a heart attack, was preventable.

From that time on I included questions about the father's weight, eating habits, etc. and suggested to mothers that it was in their best interest to know and supervise not only their children's health but their husband's too. This is a far better approach than merely sympathizing with her when he has his heart attack. I believe fathers should be healthy and alive to insure two parents per family. It was amazing how little the wives knew about their husbands.

One of the first mothers whom I questioned said that her husband ate no breakfast, no lunch and had a huge meal at night, usually at a public function of some sort. He also did not exercise and had high blood cholesterol. Her husband was on a fast track to a heart attack. By explaining the situation to her, I was able to convince her to try to help her husband make changes in his lifestyle. Fortunately, she listened as did her husband and he made the necessary changes.

DIVORCES:

A Pediatrician is interested in preserving the family for the children's sake who are usually the victims in a divorce.

After many years of counseling divorced mothers, I have attempted to analyze the causes for divorce. There seem to be three: unfaithfulness, drugs or alcohol. Even though it is difficult to convince a woman in love to consider the following questions before she marries, the answers are too important to wait until after the marriage.

In regard to faithfulness: Does he lie? What is his reputation? Are his parents divorced?

In regard to alcohol: How much alcohol does he drink now? Is his mother or father an alcoholic? Do his friends drink to excess?

In regard to drugs: Does he take drugs now? Does his family or friends use drugs?

Early in my career a mother came to my office with a sick child. The mother had bruises on her face and forearm. I asked her what had happened. She said, "My husband works on the railroad. When he finishes work he usually stops at a tavern and comes home drunk and sometimes he beats me." I was horrified and asked, "Why don't you leave him?" She replied, "Because my children are hungry". This story had a happy ending. Her husband stopped drinking and I continued to be their Pediatrician for their children and then their grandchildren for the next 30 years.

For some women whose husbands are violent or alcoholic or drug addicts, divorce is the only answer. Divorce or being a single mother leads to a pathway to a low paying job, inadequate housing and no time or energy to properly care for their children unless they have helpful family members or adequate babysitters or daycare centers so they can advance their learning to a better job.

It is always disturbing to me that wives are not more alert to the early signs or activities of their husbands' affairs. When the husband announces he wants a divorce, often she will say, "I had no idea that anything was wrong".

A Polish wife had never been able to divorce her mother. As a result her husband divorced her. Even then she still had no understanding of what had caused the divorce.

However, when a mother tells me her husband wants a divorce I talk to her and sometimes to the husband if he will come to my office. One approach I use is, "Your wife is an attractive woman. If you divorce her, she will probably remarry. Do you want another man to raise your children?"

After listening to the husband, the next step is to try to have a meeting with the husband and wife together to resolve some issues.

A wife was distraught that her husband wanted a divorce. In analyzing the facts, it seemed that her husband wanted to buy a farm and move to the country. She refused and her husband soon found a woman at work who wanted to live on a farm with him. Confronted with the possibility of divorce the wife soon realized that she would love to live on a farm. There was no divorce and they lived happily on the farm for many years.

Mr. Fisher was a super salesman. One of his customers was the female president of a large manufacturing company. They began a relationship that was more pleasure than business. Mrs. Fisher soon discovered the affair. When she confronted him with her discovery, Mr. Fisher said that he was afraid to end the affair because he might lose a large part of his income. After several intense discussion sessions, Mr. Fisher agreed to have no further contact with the other woman outside office hours.

All went well for several weeks until Mrs. Fisher called me to say that her husband was having dinner with the woman president that evening. Mrs. Fisher was both annoyed and amused but wanted to take effective action. I suggested she join them for dinner and give her husband a choice. In a pleasant and effective manner she said to her husband, "I want you to decide which one of us you want. I will be waiting in the car in the parking lot. I will give you five minutes to decide."

In a few minutes Mr. Fisher led a weeping ex-dinner companion to her car and drove home with his wife.

In our office we saw many never married or divorced mothers and they and their children were living in poverty and despair. The ex-husbands and boy friends were often not very helpful. We taught our nurses and assistants to recognize the difficulties that these mothers faced and to treat them kindly. Since some of our female employees were divorced, they understood the problem. We gave them samples of antibiotics, formula, vitamins, etc. If they did not have a way to bring their sick child to the office, I made a house call.

GRANDMOTHERS

I respect the authority that grandmothers have in a family. If a grandmother does not like you, you are doomed. She will ask sweetly, "What do you think about bellybands? I used them on all my children." The correct answer is that bellybands are unnecessary. But if I give this answer, the minute she leaves my office she will state to her daughter, "I don't believe that your doctor keeps up with the latest advances."

When an infant, a young woman and an older woman come together in my examining room, I have to be careful not to assume anything. The older woman may be the mother, the paternal grandmother, the maternal grandmother or just a friend. I listen and they eventually identify themselves.

FOREIGNERS IN MY PRACTICE

Among the married Notre Dame graduate students were many from foreign countries. The Japanese wives seemed to be the most feminine with a good relationship with their husbands and children. The Chinese students who had one child were in a constant state of despair. They wanted more than one child and knew that if they returned to China that was impossible. Consequently, many did not return to China.

The wives from India were more withdrawn and subdued. They had no status. A husband of one Indian lady who was my patient beat her regularly. She wanted a divorce. Her parents and her husband's parents came from India to try to dissuade her. They did not seem to care that she was being beaten. She divorced her husband and was ostracized by the entire South Bend India community. Her husband told their children that she was evil.

TREATING GROWN-UP CHILDREN

Because pediatricians did so many spinal taps for poliomyelitis and meningitis, we were sometimes asked to do taps on adults. One of these adults was a very frightened woman whose doctor thought she had polio. I met her and her husband in the Emergency Room. It took one hour of reassurance and persuasion to convince her that I could do the tap. As I inserted the spinal needle a thick brown fluid appeared. I thought I had obtained blood or some other fluid. But the fluid actually was spinal f luid with a few white cells and a very high protein level indicating a spinal canal block. She did not have polio. A neurosurgeon removed a small benign tumor which was compressing her spinal cord. She made a complete recovery.

One Saturday morning a mother brought her sick child for evaluation. The mother seemed very depressed and I turned my attention to her. She said that she had chronic diarrhea for months and was losing weight. Stool cultures, x-rays, blood and other lab studies and colonoscopy did not diagnose her disease and medicines had not helped. She said that she was very discouraged and was even considering suicide.

I suggested that she go home, get a baby sitter and return with her husband in the afternoon. She returned at 2PM and told me the whole history of her illness.

Pediatricians know diarrhea and I had the luxury of knowing that her previous studies had ruled out many different diseases. Celiac Disease seemed to be the probable diagnosis and I recommended that she try a gluten free diet. My wife (who is a dietitian) placed her on a regime which excluded all wheat, barley and oats. The diarrhea and cramping ceased within a few days and she gained 10 pounds in the next few months. Making the right diagnosis of celiac disease was easy because I had diagnosed and treated that disease many times in infants and children.

The increasing use of immunizations means that many childhood diseases have become uncommon and doctors may never have seen a patient with the specific disease.

I made a house call on the Voll's eleven children who were all sick with either the Mumps or measles. Mrs. Voll had brought all the beds into the living room and attached a chart to each bed. When I looked at her I said "How long have you had the Mumps?" She had gone to her internist because she had a swelling of her face. He told her that she had a tooth abscess. She went to her dentist who said that her teeth were fine. Neither the internist nor the dentist thought of Mumps.

Mumps is an inflammation of the salivary glands that consist of the parotids, the submaxillary and the sublinquals which are sometimes confused with lymph nodes. The secret to diagnosing Mumps is to look inside the mouth where the salivary glands discharge saliva. If the salivary glands are infected, the opening to the salivary ducts is inflamed.

Because Phenobarbital is readily available, it has been a favorite drug for adults attempting suicide. A doctor's wife was one such patient. She was hospitalized in a deep coma after ingesting a massive dose of Phenobarbital. Her internist told her husband that nothing could be done and that his wife might die. Her husband called me to see if I could help. From experience with children with overdoses of Phenobarbital, I knew that we needed to keep her hydrated with IV fluids and give antibiotics to prevent pneumonia.

We treated her as a big sick child. We elevated the head of her bed, ordered IV fluids for her body size, measured her intake and out put, watched for infection and had round the clock nursing care. She slept for 10 days but woke up in good physical condition just as the children had who accidentally ingested large amounts of Phenobarbital.

A few days before Christmas in 1970, my friend, Bill Leach (47 years of age) brought me a present. In a casual conversation he mentioned that he was having trouble seeing out of both sides of his eyes. He also had headaches and decreased vision. I suspected a pituitary tumor. Since his daughter had an eye appointment scheduled for the next day, I suggested that he take her appointment instead.

The ophthalmologist confirmed my suspicion and sent him to the Cleveland Clinic. The surgeon removed a cystic pituitary tumor on January 8, 1971. The doctor sent him home on Dilantin and Cortisone.

On New Year's Eve in 1965 we went to a party in our neighborhood. Since we were going to a ski resort early the next morning, we had packed our station wagon with skis, clothing and my medicine bag. As we arrived at the party a guest, who had left the party earlier, phoned the host to say in a very weak voice, "I don't feel very well" Our host, who was a Radiologist, and I thought we had best make a house call immediately. We jumped in my station wagon and 2 minutes later we walked in to his house. We found the man lying barely conscious on the floor in a bathroom. He mumbled he had a sore throat and that he had taken a teaspoon of his son's medicine. We observed a bottle of liquid penicillin in the bathroom and it was obvious that he was in anaphylactic shock.

Fortunately I had my medical bag with me and quickly injected Epinephrine, Decadron and Penicillinase IV. We did not move him and called for an ambulance. We had some difficulty convincing the authorities that this was not a drunk on New Year's Eve but a real emergency. The man spent a week in the hospital and made a complete recovery. He knows that he wants no further relationship with penicillin. I don't blame him.

Richard Trenkner was the Administrator of Memorial Hospital. When he caught Mumps from his sons, he asked me to treat him too. He developed all of the possible complications of Mumps: pancreatitis, orchitis and encephalitis. Because of his vomiting, I gave him IV fluids at home and visited him daily.

On the fourth day of his illness, I asked if he thought I should admit him to the hospital. He looked at me and said, "I'm too sick to go the hospital". Like 99% of Mumps patients, he made a complete recovery.

I received a frantic call from the mother of one of my now grown-up ex-patients who was a stockbroker in New York City. He had been ill for several weeks with fatigue and fever. He had been examined and tested with no specific disease diagnosed. His mother asked if I would examine if he came home to South Bend. I agreed to do so.

Lyme Disease had been considered in his differential diagnosis but the tests were negative and deer ticks were certainly unusual in Manhattan. The possibility of the correct diagnosis was revealed by one of my first questions,." Where did you spend your summer vacation?" His reply, 'in Wisconsin". After that the diagnosis was easy. Further tests were positive for Lyme Disease. I treated him with Ceftrixone and he made a complete recovery.

Nights when I was not on call, I did not answer my phone after 10 PM. The Answering Service took the calls and referred them to the doctor on call. That didn't stop my patients. They knew where we lived. One time a child came to the door and said, "My mother says you should come right away". I drove the boy back to his home two blocks away. His father was in an upstairs bathroom, bleeding from a scalp laceration. I stopped the bleeding and phoned for an ambulance because he obviously had lost a lot of blood. I followed the ambulance. In the Emergency Room, I sewed up the laceration and arranged for admission and probable blood transfusion. As I drove his wife home at 2 AM with both of us in our pajamas with a few odd garments covering them, I hoped a policeman didn't decide to stop us for some reason. The explanation would have been difficult.

37. WEDDINGS

Weddings are an important part of the life of a Pediatrician. Why? Female infants become little girls and little girls grow up. The Pediatrician has been a good friend to many girls growing up and she wants him at her wedding.

In the wedding season, which means May, June, August, and December, I would often have 3-4 weddings to attend on a single Saturday. This required a tight schedule. We would go to one wedding ceremony, skip the reception to make the next ceremony. One Saturday, my wife and I had skimmed through parts of three ceremonies and receptions and faced a fourth. My wife begged off. I debated whether I had the energy to attend the fourth but decided to go. I arrived as the last two or three guests stood in the receiving line. The bride spotted me and cried out, "Oh! Dr. Erickson is here" and hugged me. During the reception the father came up to me six times to thank me for coming. The bride was special to me because she was a seizure patient under control with medication. Could I have made a decision not to go to her wedding?

At another wedding, I called to tell the girl that I could not attend after all. I was treating a very sick patient in the hospital. The next day she brought me a piece of her wedding cake, a bottle of champagne and a video of her wedding.

One of the most beautiful weddings we attended was at the Sacred Heart Cathedral on the Notre Dame campus with Father Ted Hesburgh as the celebrant. The reception was held at the Stephan Center to which we were bussed on a cold winter night. Andy Frame ushers from Chicago handled the crowd. Even they were impressed as I checked my wife's and my coats. They said "Wow!" I said,
"This is just an ordinary Friday night wedding in South Bend".

Artificial carpeting had been laid over the cement floor. The Lester Lannin band was playing continuously on a revolving stage in the center of the room while dozens of attendants rushed hither and yon with food and drink.

For another wedding I waited 22 years. When Elizabeth was born she was normal. But when she was a year old she developed a retinoblastoma of her right eye. If the eye were not removed, the cancer would spread. Her parents took her to the Eye Hospital at Columbia University in New York City where the eye was removed. She had an artificial eyeball installed and grew up a normal girl with no complications.

At each office visit I would tell her how beautiful she was – and she was – and that I looked forward to dancing with her at her wedding. When she was nineteen years old she had a new artificial eyeball installed which was attached to her eye muscles so that the new eye would move with her normal eye. Now she was even more beautiful. She was graduated from Notre Dame and soon fell in love and became engaged to a fine young man.

At her wedding reception, her father came over to my table and said," Elizabeth is ready for her dance." We danced the dance I had anticipated for 22 years. Elizabeth, her father and I shed a few tears.

Sometimes, getting to the church is not easy. Susie was an honor graduate from Notre Dame. She became pregnant and had a baby by her live-in lawyer boyfriend. Because I had been her doctor since the day she was born, I talked to her quite frankly. She said that her boyfriend was not ready for marriage. Neither was he ready to pay any bills for his baby's care. Susie had another baby with her boy friend. I again urged marriage but marriage was not on his agenda.

Susie had a third baby. This time I screamed and jumped up and down but the boy friend was not ready. Three months after the third baby was born, the boy friend told Susie he was sick of babies and asked her to move out— which she did. I continued to provide medical care and immunizations to Susie's three children. Within a year, Susie met a suitable man who wanted to marry her. I attended her wedding at St. Mary's College chapel with her three children playing happily at the back of the church. As far as I know, they lived happily ever after.

We went to wedding receptions at country clubs, social clubs, in homes and in back yards. We could expect the same format at the social halls whether they were at the Catholic Church or Polish or Hungarian halls. The parishioners covered the long tables with white paper on which were placed coconut cream, banana cream, and chocolate cream pies. The men gathered at the bar in the corner where beer and mixed drinks were served. Wine was not a favorite beverage. Soft drinks were available for the children who were always welcomed at the receptions.

After the priest arrived to bless the food, the waiters and waitresses (usually children of the parish) brought in the food prepared by the women of the parish. The menu was always the same: platters of fried chicken and Polish sausage, bowls of mashed potatoes, string beans, sweet and sour cabbage, and noodles with chicken gravy. Periodically, someone would bang their spoon on the glass, a signal for the newlyweds to kiss.

When everyone had finished, the tables were cleared. Then the dancing began. The children had the most fun. The boys ran around, the girls danced together or with their mother or father. The bride danced with various male partners who stuffed dollar bills and checks in her white satin pouch.

38. TEACHING THE DOCTORS

As Director of Pediatric Medical Education for the Family Practice Residents and medical students at Memorial Hospital in South Bend, I gave hundreds of lectures.

One of my teaching points was:

Rule out organic diseases before labeling an illness as psychological.

A one year old infant would not eat solid food. Whenever she was fed solid food, she vomited. Several pediatricians told the mother that the problem was psychological because the infant would drink liquids without difficulty.

The first step in evaluating the infant was to take a chest x-ray. The x-rays showed a gold baby ring imbedded halfway down the esophagus. Liquids could flow freely past the ring but when the mother fed solid food, the ring tipped and filled with food and the baby vomited. Following surgical removal of the ring, the so-called psychological vomiting stopped.

The lesson is: "Never put a ring on a baby's finger. It will never stay there."

Another infant with the same vomiting problem had an apple seed caught in her esophagus.

One of my favorite patients was Timmy, a 10 year old boy with abdominal pain who had been examined in my office or who had been examined in the Emergency Room 24 different times but no disease was found. One morning at 6 AM his mother telephoned me to report that her son was having another attach of severe tummy pain. I met Timmy and his mother in my office at 7AM. My examination revealed a distended abdomen with visible loops of intestines indicating an obstruction. An hour later in the operating room, we found the cause of his abdominal pain. He had an internal hernia. A loop of small intestine had slipped through an opening where the duodenum was retroperitoneal. In the past, a loop of the small intestine would slip through this space but then slip out by itself. This time the loop of intestine did not release. The surgeon had to remove 6 feet of jejunum.

Elsie was a 12 year old girl with chest pain. Her chest X-Rays were normal and so were her heart studies. Because the pain was over the right lower rib cage, gallbladder disease was considered but the tests were negative. We found that she had slipping rib syndrome. This is a sprain disorder caused by an injury to the coastal cartilages of the 8th, 9th, and 10th ribs. These cartilages are attached to each other by fibrous tissues. If this fibrous tissue is disrupted, the anterior end of the cartilage pulls away and rubs against the inside of the rib above. Pain is caused by irritation of the adjacent intercostals nerve. We referred Elsie to a thoracic surgeon who removed the 10th costal cartilage and relieved her pain.

All of these patients had been evaluated by different doctors who thought that the patient or the mother had psychological reasons for their difficulties.

Karen was a twenty-year-old college student who developed severe headaches. She had been evaluated at the college infirmary and was sent home with a diagnosis of a possible brain tumor because of her increased spinal fluid pressure. This was before the days of scans and Magnetic Imaging. The next step in her evaluation would have been a pneumoencephalogram but I was reluctant to have this done.

Karen told me that she was taking 500 mgm of tetracycline three times daily prescribed by her dermatologist. I had just read an article in the Journal of Pediatrics by Dr. Stuart and Dr. Litt titled "Tetracycline-Associated Intracranial Hypertension in an Adolescent: A Complication of Systemic Acne Therapy"

When I discontinued her tetracycline her headaches went away and her spinal fluid pressure returned to normal. She was happily married two years later.

Today we can rule out brain tumors or other intracranial causes of severe headache with an MRI.

LISTENING

One of my favorite lectures was teaching the doctors the rules of being a good physician for children.

The first rule is: listen to the mother.

I learned a valuable lesson in the first few months of practice. One morning a mother brought her six week old male infant to the Emergency Room because he had a slight fever. His physical exam and lab tests were normal. However, at the mother's insistence, I admitted the baby to the hospital. At noon I examined him again and still could find nothing unusual. At five PM I returned to the hospital and decided to do a lumbar puncture. As I was inserting the needle, I thought to myself, "Why am I doing this?" The spinal fluid dripped out thick and full of white cells. The infant had meningitis.

The mother gets full credit for diagnosing a sick infant. After ten days of antibiotics, the infant made a complete recovery. He was my first meningitis case in private practice—which I had not overlooked—thanks to his mother.

Infants with colic are often dismissed with words of assurance that nothing is wrong. However, some of these infants may have an inquinal hernia, an ear infection or some other treatable problem

A mother had taken her colicky infant to several doctors without relief. Her husband and mother-in-law thought that there was nothing wrong except an inadequate mother. I watched her infant for an entire afternoon. The infant had severe paroxysms of pain. X-rays revealed a malrotation of the intestines which surgery soon relieved.

The second rule: listen to the nurses.

Fever of unknown origin led to hospitalization of a sixteen year old girl. The cause was easily discovered. While the nurse was taking her temperature, the girl quickly went into the bathroom where she held the thermometer under the hot water faucet.

A doctor from Goshen, Indiana referred a one day old male infant to me. The infant was lethargic, opisthotonic and vomiting. The mother's previous newborn had the same symptoms but died at 3 days of age with no diagnosis. Her second newborn was acting the same way. I did a lumbar puncture and started him on IV fluids. A pediatric nurse said to me, "The urine smells funny." This was the clue we needed to make the diagnosis of Maple Sugar Urine Disease. We continued the IV fluids and started him on a formula free of leucine, isoleucine and valine, three amino acids that his body could not process. The first newborn died because those three amino acids accumulated in his brain and other tissues. Because of the nurse's observation of the second newborn we were able to prevent brain damage to this baby before it occurred. By following a special diet and formula that eliminated the three amino acids, the infant could live a normal life.

A Pediatrician from Elkhart, Indiana referred a six month old female infant to our hospital. The infant had a fever and was dehydrated. As a trained pediatric nurse and I were evaluating the infant and preparing to start IV fluids, the infant urinated. The intelligent nurse said, "The baby has diabetes" and she was right.

Diabetes is the only condition that I know where a dehydrated infant or child will continue to urinate. The hyperosmolality of the urine is due to the high blood sugar drawing the fluid out of the kidneys.

A teenage girl was admitted to the hospital with seizures. All studies including electroencephalograms were normal. A child may have seizures and still have a normal EEG but the clinical manifestations of the seizures were strange. I asked a student nurse to talk with the patient and find out what her problem was. The nurse reported that the girl wanted to talk with me.

The patient said that the seizures began shortly after the girl's stepfather made sexual advances toward her. I assured the girl that she did not have seizures.

I explained to the mother and stepfather that something terrible had happened to their daughter but she would not tell me what it was. I told her, "If anything like that happened to her in the future that the girl was to telephone me immediately." The stepfather "got the message" and seemed sufficiently scared to not harass the girl again.

There was a three year old boy who really did have seizures. His mother brought him to my office with the history that several doctors had not been able to control his convulsions. For some reason I did not trust the mother. I admitted the boy to the hospital and ordered blood calcium, glucose and other chemistries. I asked the nurse to carefully observe the boy and his mother. There was nothing unusual until the third day. The nurse reported that the boy said to her, "Mummy gives me Daddy's shot" The diagnosis of the cause for the convulsions was easy after that bit of information. The child's father had diabetes and the mother was giving her son injections of her husband's insulin, which caused hypoglycemic convulsions.

Why was the mother doing this? She was a psychopath and for some strange reason needed her son to have a problem so that she could get attention. She had even gone to the newspaper to report that no one would help her son. After explaining the situation to the news reporter and asking him to give the mother no publicity, the social worker and I were able to get the mother the help she needed. The injections stopped and so did the seizures.

Third rule: Listen to the grandmother

A grandmother, whom I knew, brought her five year old granddaughter to my office. I asked her the question I always ask the parents or children, "Why are you here?" To which she replied, "Because I think my granddaughter has leukemia."

There was nothing in the child's history to suggest leukemia and her physical examination was normal. I ordered a blood count anyway. The child did have leukemia.

This office visit occurred many years ago but it taught me not to be surprised at anything and to listen to anyone who wanted me to listen.

Fourth rule: Listen to yourself

A mother brought her seven year old boy to the Emergency Room because the boy had suddenly gone blind. This was his third trip to the ER. I was disturbed that the other two doctors had not made the diagnosis. When I took his blood pressure, the diagnosis was easy. He had hypertensive encephalography secondary to acute glomerulonephritis. I admitted him to the hospital, placed him on anti-hypertensive drugs and asked the nurses to watch him closely. His blood pressure and his urine returned to normal. His sight returned and he made a complete recovery.

Twenty years ago, rheumatic fever and glomerulonephritis were two sequelae of strep infection. Today, penicillin and other antibiotics keep these sequelae from occurring.

A week later, a mother brought her son to my office. The boy complained of a headache. His blood pressure was slightly elevated and I reassured the mother that he was probably under stress. After they left the office, I realized I should have done a urinalysis to rule out nephritis. I frantically telephoned the mother and asked her to bring her son back for a urinalysis. The urine showed he had nephritis. Even though I should have thought of nephritis immediately, I was not listening to myself. I had no right to be critical of the other doctors.

Fifth rule: Be a skeptic.

One of the first patients that I examined in private practice was a girl with headaches and vomiting. I referred her to a local neurosurgeon. He tried to reassure me that the girl did not have a brain tumor, but I was not convinced. Since there were no Scans or MRIs to rule brain tumors out at that time and because I had just finished training near Boston, I sent her to a neurosurgeon at Children's Hospital in Boston, Massachusetts. The Boston neurosurgeon excised a small frontal lobe tumor and the girl returned home to South Bend without headaches or vomiting.

I was suspicious that a three year old boy had megacolon. Children with megacolon have a section of their colon that lacks the ganglions of the mysenteric plexus, the section of nerves that propel the feces along the colon. The section of the colon proximal to the obstruction becomes very distended hence the name, megacolon. The result is extreme constipation. The diagnosis is made by doing a rectal biopsy to see if the colon lacks the necessary nerve cells in a specific area. Then this defective area of the colon can be removed and the working areas of the colon can be sewed back together.

The biopsy report from the local pathology lab reported there were numerous Meissner ganglionic plexi present on the slides. This meant that I was wrong and the child did not have megacolon.

When the child's constipation continued, I sent the boy and his slides to Children's Memorial Hospital in Chicago. Dr. Joseph Boggs, the pathologist there, looked at the slides and said, "There are no ganglions of the mysenteric plexus on these slides". Dr. Orvar Swenson, the surgeon who had invented the pull-through operation for megacolon, operated successfully on the child.

This episode taught me that not all laboratory or pathology reports are correct and for me to have the courage of my convictions.

A ten year old girl had bouts of severe abdominal pain. In addition to other studies I ordered an upper GI series with a small bowel follow-through to rule out malrotation of the intestines. The local Radiologist read the x-rays as normal. I was suspicious and sent the girl and her x-rays to Riley Hospital in Indianapolis, Indiana. There the x-rays showed there was malrotation. Dr. Jay Grosfeld performed the surgery and relieved the girl of abdominal pain.

When I was just starting private practice I examined a six-week-old male infant whom I had diagnosed as having pyloric stenosis. He had a classic history of projectile vomiting with weight loss. I could feel the olive size pylorus and observe the reverse peristalysis. But the x-rays did not confirm my diagnosis. The surgeon I consulted agreed with my diagnosis. When the x-ray doctor found out that we thought he was wrong, he was adamant that surgery should not be performed. On the day of surgery, we asked the x-ray doctor to be present in the operating room. We showed him the pyloric mass and even let him feel it. The surgeon removed the obstruction giving the baby complete relief.

In defense of the roentgenologist, at that time Lipiodal was used as the material for the baby to swallow to prove pyloric stenosis. Lipiodal was too slick and oily to delineate the obstruction in this infant. Needless to say, after that, barium was used instead of lipiodal

My last rule: Consider what purpose the illness may serve for the child or parent. Does the child or parent want the problem to be solved?

Finally, be careful what is said. Words can be like scalpels. Words can cut and damage but when used effectively, they can also heal.

39. MODERN PEDIATRICS

Nowadays, one of the best features of pediatrics is that few patients die. Better obstetrical care delivers newborns in good physical condition. Congenital heart problems and other abnormalities are uncommon. Immunizations have prevented many diseases.

What I am saying is that since few children die, we pediatricians do not know how to handle death. When a child dies under my care, I feel guilty and very inadequate. I wonder what I missed or should have done differently.

But accidents are taking a toll on our children. One mother had two daughters aged 14 and 16 years of age respectively. One daughter died in a drunken car accident and the second died a year later under the same circumstances. If only teenagers would stop drinking and driving, the life of a pediatrician would be much easier.

A distraught mother phoned me to tell me that her 21 year old son had been murdered. He had been my patient since birth and had been living in an apartment with his girlfriend. They had been quarreling. His girlfriend called a male acquaintance and asked him to rescue her because she was being held against her wishes. Several young men came to her rescue. A fight began outside the apartment with pushing and shoving. My patient staggered back up to his apartment and 30 minutes later he was dead. One of the rescuers had punched the victim in the chest. It was not a severe blow but he held a small pen knife in his fist and severed an artery.

The mother and I had several discussions and I did my best to help her deal with the death of her only son.

The situation became more complex for me when another patient of mine appeared. He had been the one who had delivered the fatal punch. This 17 year old young man and his family were frantic. No one had anticipated murder as the outcome of a minor squabble. I evaluated both sides of a horrible event and tried to give advice and comfort to each family. The tragedy was intensified because one boy was white and the other was black.

Another near-tragedy occurred soon afterwards. An 18 year old young man was delivering pizza for Papa Johns. He rang the doorbell but there was no answer. As he turned to leave he was hit on the back of the head by a brick. He fell to the ground and a second robber shot him in the chest. Thirty minutes later when he was brought to the Emergency Room, I examined the deliveryman. The bullet had hit his sternum and lodged just near a rib. There was no heart or lung damage. He went home the next day and the surgeons removed the bullet several weeks later. One robber was arrested and went to jail. He claimed not to have shot the man but he refused to identify the one who did.

Was alcohol or drugs a factor in these tragedies? I think so. I learned that often when fathers were difficult and critical of my care of their children that alcohol was a factor. When there were family problems, physical child or mother abuse, I found it wise to ask about alcohol or drug use by the mother or father.

INTERFERENCE WITH A DOCTOR'S JUDGMENT

In recent years some of my time and energy has been spent fighting the rules and restrictions of the HMOs and health insurance companies.

Jennifer was a 10 year old girl who came to my office at 11 AM with a 3 day history of abdominal pain. Her abdomen was very tender in the right lower quadrant. Her history and abdominal findings indicated that she had an acutely inflamed appendix. Since I had been her physician from the time she was born, I knew that she had coarctation of the aorta, which was surgically repaired at 3 days of age. If the appendix ruptured the bacteria might settle on the site of the repaired aorta. She needed an immediate appendectomy. I phoned a surgeon, explained the problem and sent Jennifer to the hospital. The surgeon phoned me at 2 PM to say that the appendix was gangrenous and at the point of rupture and he removed it in time to prevent complications. Jennifer left the hospital in 3 days and was soon back at school.

The insurance company said, "We will not pay her hospital expenses because you did not ask our permission to admit her and you did not get a second opinion."

If I had followed the insurance company's rules, Jennifer's appendix would have ruptured and she might have developed bacterial endocarditis and would have spent at least two weeks in the hospital with antibiotic, gastric tubes and IV fluids. Not only would this have been very expensive for the insurance company but would be very traumatic for the child and family.

Whenever I had a mentally retarded child as a patient, it was my custom to continue being his physician as long as he lived. My rationalization was that I knew the patient and his problems better than a new doctor would. The real reason was that I became very attached to them.

Sam had viral encephalitis in infancy and was left with severe brain damage. His mother devoted her life to him and he survived many critical illnesses. When he was 43 years of age I hospitalized him with asthmatic bronchitis. He improved in the hospital but he was very frightened of the needles and procedures of the hospital environment. His mother and I decided that he would do better at home and I discharged him after 3 days. Within a week he was fully recovered.

Several months later I received a letter from Medicaid accusing me of failure to provide proper care by discharging a patient while he still had a fever. Usually I do not react to letters from Review Board members but I felt compelled to write them a letter: "When someone sitting in an office several hundred miles away can better determine the care of a patient than the doctor sitting a the patients' bedside, then it is time to change the way you judge quality of care."

Several months later I received another letter from Medicaid. It read: "Forget the previous letter."

It is difficult enough for a physician to learn when to admit and when to discharge a patient from the hospital let alone someone far away on the insurance review board to think they can do it better than the patient's MD.

James H., a 15 year old boy was sent to our Emergency Room. He had lost 10 pounds in the past week and was comatose. He was dehydrated and in respiratory distress. His blood sugar was over 1000 (Normal is 100). After giving him IV insulin and fluids in the ER for several hours, he improved enough to be transferred to the Pediatric Ward. By the next morning, he was out of his coma with a normal blood sugar. The regulation of his insulin dosage and teaching of proper future diabetic management now began.

James and his parents had to learn how to test his blood and urine for sugar, how to provide the proper diet, how to detect signs of low or high blood sugar, how and when to inject insulin.

After 7 days in the hospital, James had gained 5 pounds and was stable with blood sugars in good normal ranges so that he could be referred back to his family doctor. We felt that our staff and his parents had done a good job.

The insurance company review doctor felt otherwise. He said that we should have sent James home in 3 days. I asked the doctor if he had ever treated a child in diabetic coma. He said that he never had.

If we were careless enough to send James home in 3 days after being in a diabetic coma, we would not have been practicing first class medicine.

Insurance companies try to play games with children's lives. Doctors do not.

40. PEOPLE WHO MAKE A DIFFERENCE

The people who made the most difference in my life are my wife and children.

It probably was different and difficult for my children to grow up in a pediatric family. I was both their father and their doctor. If they needed sutures, I sewed them up. If they were sick, I examined and treated them. I trusted them and they trusted me. The only time we had a problem was when my teenage daughters snuck off to a dermatologist to have their ears pierced. They knew I wouldn't approve. But at least they went to a doctor.

Thanksgiving, Christmas and Birthdays were always big events. Each child planned the menu for their birthdays resulting in some strange meals.

Their mother and I spent many hours for many years attending swim meets in which our children participated. Quincy and Robin were voted most valuable swimmer for their teams. Quincy became the captain of her Jackson High School team which won the city championship. Gary coached the Swanson Highlands team to a summer championship.

Each winter we looked forward to skiing for a week in Michigan or New England. Each summer we drove in our station wagon east to the homes of the grandparents or west to Pediatric meetings. Our biggest adventure was a round trip train trip through the Grand Canyon and Santa Fe to Los Angeles and back by the northern route. But too soon the children grew up and took summer jobs.

Every 3-4 years our summer project was painting the outside of the house. No one fell off the scaffolding and everyone participated without too much grumbling. We lived in the same house for 42 years so it was painted many times.

The childhood years ended too soon and one by one each child went off to college; Gary to Dartmouth, Robin to Syracuse and Quincy to Purdue.

Looking back I realize that we really had 5 children. Annette Juntgen, an Exchange Student from Germany lived with us for a year when Robin was a senior in high school. Valerie Wood who lived next door ate more meals with us and spent more time with us than she did at home.

The happiest years of my life were when my children were growing and living at home. I was thankful that they escaped serious illness and accidents and thankful that they are now happily married with children of their own. What gives me great satisfaction is that their mother and I can continue to be part of their lives.

The memories are priceless.

Painting the house in 1965: G. Walter, Gary, Martha, Quincy, and Robin.

Martha and G. Walter Erickson's Fiftieth Anniversary with the family.

*First row (left to right): Herrick Erickson-Brigl, Arianna Nagle, Molly Gebrian,
Eric Gebrian, Jason Erickson, and Christopher Erickson.*
*Second row: Quincy Erickson and Stephen Nagle, Jeffrey and Robin Gebrian, Martha and
Rick Erickson, Carol and Garwood Erickson.*

HEROES

Other individuals stand out because influence on my life.

A child who lived 10 miles away in the country needed a house call. Because I was at the hospital with seriously sick children, I asked the mother if she could bring her child to the hospital. There was a light snow that turned into a blizzard by the time the mother arrived with her sick child in her arms. When I asked her how she got there, she said she hitched hiked. This was no big deal for this mother who had been in a concentration camp in Germany. She still had her identification number tattooed on her forearm. I drove her home.

A mother who wasn't too intelligent herself brought her mentally retarded daughter to me for routine health care. She told me that she had another child in a Home for Retarded Children in Fort Wayne. One day she came to my office very excited. She told me that she had a third child when she was an unmarried teenager. She had given that child up for adoption. She said that she knew the family who had adopted him but she had no contact with her son or the adopting parents. However, she learned that her son was being graduated from high school. His father was not the father of the retarded children. Her first child was normal, president of the senior class, and going to college. She said, "I sat in the back of the auditorium. I didn't tell anyone why I was there. I cried. I was so proud."

That mother was one of my heroes.

Another of my heroes was Reverend Hamel, pastor or the Broadway Methodist Church. His children were patients of mine. When he brought them to my office he would tell everyone in the waiting room what a great doctor I was. No wonder I liked him. Because he loved fire engines, he became the official chaplain of the Fire Department. Whenever there was a fire, he went to the scene and counseled and comforted the victims.

When I discovered that some of my patients were not attending school because the family had to share the same pair of shoes or boots, I called Reverend Hamel. He talked to the congregation and to some shoe stores and established a Shoe Bank at his church. After that whenever I found a child whose shoes and finances were inadequate, I wrote a prescription to the Shoe Bank.

Shoes have always represented wealth to me. When I was a senior in college, I did not own a decent pair of shoes. Mine were work shoes covered with paint and grime. I was reluctant to accept invitations to private homes for dinner because I did not own another pair of shoes. When my children were growing up I always cleaned and polished theirs as well as mine.

I love white grandmothers but I stand in awe of black grandmothers. They raised half of the black children who have been my patients. The mothers of these babies are often unmarried teenagers doing the best they can with situations mostly beyond their control.

I remember fondly, Mrs. Jennings, a black grandmother who gathered every sick child from the west side of South Bend to bring them to my office. She never left until she had conned me out of all formula, vitamins, diapers, and other samples that we had in stock. She was an angel. She labored full time caring for hers and everyone else's grandbabies. She had high blood pressure, little money and a big heart. She died in her early fifties. She was another of my heroes.

PEOPLE IN THE PUBLIC EYE

Otis Bowen, MD

An individual for whom I have great respect is Otis Bowen, MD. While practicing in Bremen, Indiana, he referred sick children to me at Memorial Hospital. He went on to be a State Senator and then Governor of Indiana. My wife, as a Republican worker, worked to get him elected Governor of Indiana. Our daughter, Quincy, was a page for him when he was in the Indiana legislature. President Ronald Reagan appointed him Secretary of Health and Human Services.

When he was Governor, he appointed me to the Governing Board of Northern Indiana Children's Hospital. While he was governor, a law was passed that forbid compensation in malpractice lawsuits to exceed $100,000.00, which has resulted in keeping malpractice insurance for the doctors at a minimum. For over 50 years Otis Bowen has been an inspiration and a model of greatness for what a man could be as a physician and as a citizen and as a friend.

Father Theodore Hesburgh

Father Theodore Hesburgh came to Notre Dame in 1950 when he was Chaplain to the students in Vetville. While I administered to the children's illnesses, Father Hesburgh handled their spiritual needs. I also was the pediatrician for his brother, Jim's children and grandchildren. For over 50 years Father Hesburgh and I have had conversations at christenings, weddings, football games, meetings, and funerals. I was honored when he gave the invocation at my retirement dinner.

Hundreds of other South Bend physicians and clergymen should be mentioned here. These are the people who hold a community together.

Jean and Van Gates

Jean and Van Gates are our best friends and I have been the pediatrician for their children and grandchildren. As the South Bend Chevrolet dealer, Van has provided employment for hundreds of families through the years. Both Jean and Van are community leaders involved in dozens of projects benefiting their community and their church.

Virginia and William Voll

Bill Voll was President of the Sibley Foundry. He was involved with St Joseph Hospital, Notre Dame and community development. Ginnie and he have 11 children, all of whom through the years needed house calls and lots of medical care. They were gracious enough to invite us to their children's weddings.

Jean and Glenn Gordon

Glenn Gordon was president of Studebaker-Packard and Chairman of the Board at Memorial Health Systems. Jean and he have four children who were my patients and my friends. Even though their daughter, Caroline, developed diabetes at the young age of fourteen she led a full life until the age of 53.

Mary and William Carleton

Bill Carleton was involved with Armco Steel and CEO of Tower Federal Savings Bank. His most important community work was when he was Chairman of the Board of Directors of Memorial Hospital. From 1970 to 1990 he was the catalyst who changed Memorial from a good community hospital to a great medical center. The Carleton name should be enshrined somewhere in Memorial Hospital.

Nancy Butler

Nancy Butler is Mary Lou Leighton's daughter and like family to us. She moved back to Niles, Michigan, was divorced, overcame some major illnesses, successfully raised five children and started her own real estate firm. All of her children and grandchildren live within a few miles of each other.

NOTABLE PATIENTS

Andy Granatelli

Andy Granatelli moved to South Bend to be head of the STP division of Studebaker. His wife was Dolly and his son was Anthony. They lived in a house in Twyckenham Hills several blocks away.

Andy was away many weeks at a time and Dolly began cooking and freezing foods for Andy's return. One Christmas morning when I made a house call for a sick Anthony, she served me a stack of Swedish pancakes and a large piece of Dutch apple pie.

After another house call on a summer evening, I noted smoke coming out of the garage. I called for Dolly and we used a hose to put out the fire caused by used charcoal that had been simmering in a barrel. Dolly was on the phone with Andy who was in California. She said, "I'm sorry Andy. I have to hang up. The garage is on fire!"

Andy sponsored an STP car in the Indianapolis 500 for many years. As Andy's guests we went to the time trials and met many of the drivers and their wives.

For the 500 Race we flew down on the Studebaker plane or rode in a chartered bus from South Bend to Indianapolis. We had seats in the Paddock across from the finish line. Before the Race the men guests wandered freely through Gasoline Alley and the infield. On the nights before the race Andy hosted dinner and entertainment for a large group of friends and Studebaker officials. I often missed the entertainment because a child of some member of the group would have an emergency. I remember examining a child for appendicitis on a mechanic bench in Gasoline Alley or watching the son of the Studebaker pilot who hit his head on the motel diving board.

I have stood on the Race Track just before the Race started and watched the drivers get in their cars. You could feel the charisma surrounding them as they made their way through the spectators.

I was there when the Pace Car veered off the track and toppled the viewing stand filled with writers and photographers. I was there when the Studebaker turbine race car failed at 497 miles while leading the pack. I was there when Mario Andretti finally won the 500 for Andy Granatelli and STP.

The fun and glamour ended for me when Race Driver Jimmy Clark was killed in a race in Germany. I had been with him during several Indy 500s. He was not just a picture in the newspaper. He was a man whom I knew and respected. After that I lost my interest in auto racing.

Mike deBlumenthal

Mike deBlumenthal was the Chief Engineer at Studebaker and since his daughter Lisa was my patient, he let me borrow the new Avanti car to make house calls in the evenings before the Avanti was on the market.

Sherwood Egbert

Sherwood Egbert was the president of Studebaker then and the Avanti, designed by Raymond Loew. was expected to lead Studebaker out of its financial dilemma. The only problem was that Sherwood Egbert developed carcinoma of the bile ducts and was operated on at the Lahey Clinic in Boston.

The Studebaker Board of Directors was meeting at that time and voted not to introduce and manufacture the Avanti.

I believe that if Sherwood Egbert had been healthy he could have persuaded the Directors otherwise. The Avanti was a great car and might have revived the Studebaker Corporation.

When Studebaker did fail, L. O. Gates, Van Gates father, and Paul Gilbert restored South Bend's morale with their slogan: "This is South Bend, Indiana not Studebaker, Indiana."

Ronald Como

In 1963 Ronald Como, Junior was born in St. Joseph Hospital. His father was Ronald Como and his grandfather was Perry Como. Ronald, developed Respiratory Distress Syndrome and required oxygen and special care.

Perry and his wife flew up from Florida and stayed for a week while Ron was critically ill. I phoned Dr. Lawton who was Physician-in-Chief at Children's Memorial Hospital in Chicago. I told Dr. Lawton that I thought the infant was too sick to be transferred but that I needed help. Dr. Lawton asked Dr. Hardy who was in charge of the Outpatient Clinics at Children's Hospital, to come to South Bend.

Dr. Hardy examined the baby and agreed with our treatment. In talking with Perry Como, Dr. Hardy realized that he had been the physician for the baby's father when he was born in Chicago 24 years before.

Fortunately, the baby improved and was discharged home in good condition. I reported to Perry each night for several weeks until I could assure him that the baby was out of danger.

For several years I had the fun of attending the dress rehearsals of the Kraft Music Hall at McCormick Place in Chicago. Perry Como had a relaxed personality as an entertainer but he was exhausted after a performance.

Wendy and Paige, Perry's granddaughters, were very talented singers. Their mother, Melanie, formed a group known as "The Company" which gave many performances in the Northern Indiana area.

My daughter, Robin, baby sat for the Como children. Her claim to fame came when Perry, who was visiting at the time, fixed her hair for her Senior Prom.

Wendy sang at my Retirement Dinner.

Ara Parseghian

Among my patients were two of Ara Parseghian's granddaughters who lived in South Bend. He was a great coach and a great man but he showed his real greatness when ten years ago he started a foundation to find the cause, cure and prevention for Niemann-Pick Disease. His grandchildren, who were children of his son, Mike, developed Type 3. This is a disease where cholesterol accumulates in nerve tissue leading to severe disability and death.

I hope the researchers find a cure soon.

The Morris Family

Ernest Morris formed the Associates Investment Company in South Bend in 1944. He had two daughters, May Lou and Ernestine. Mary Lou married Robert Oare and Ernestine married Mike Carmichael.

Robert Oare would certainly have become a US Senator . I remember him walking down the aisle of the First Presbyterian Church in South Bend arm-in-arm with Nelson Rockefeller. He died in an airplane crash in Tell City, Indiana in 1960.

Mike Carmichael died of a heart attack one year after he sold Associates to Gulf and Western.

Mary Lou married Judd Leighton and Ernestine married Robert Raclin.

It was my privilege to have been the pediatrician for all of the children, grandchildren and some of the great grandchildren of these two families. Their philanthropy has benefited Notre Dame, St. Mary's College, Indiana University, Memorial Hospital and the city of South Bend.

UNIVERSITY FACULTY

Notre Dame University, St. Mary's College and the Indiana University South Bend Campus all had many faculty members whose children were patients of mine. It was intellectually stimulating to be involved with these professors.

Ralph McInerny Of Notre Dame wrote the Father Dowling mysteries. These stories were later the basis for a television series.

Timothy O'Meara was the Provost of Notre Dame. I met his children the first day he began at Notre Dame. When he became Provost, I remember telling his wife that she should not run around in jeans and sneakers anymore.

41. WE GET LETTERS

During 50 years of pediatric practice I have received many letters from patients. Some letters were not kind or complimentary but most letters were thank you notes for the care of their children. These kind letters always seemed to come at the right time when I was depressed because of serious illness or the death of a child.

My favorite letter was a crudely hand printed postcard received from an Hispanic mother. The card read:

"I have faith in 3 things –
God, the Gas Company and Dr. Erickson"

I was proud to be after God but I was not sure about the Gas Company.

42. CHANGES IN THE CARE OF CHILDREN OVER MY LIFETIME

Although Poliomyelitis was the most dramatic disease that could be prevented by immunization during the period from 1950-2000, many other vaccines have since become available.

Smallpox was eliminated worldwide several years before 1950. Diphtheria, pertussis and tetanus (DPT) immunizations were in increasingly great use in the nineteen-fifties. Diphtheria is now unknown in the United States with only 2 cases in 1999 and none so far in 2000. Tetanus still occurs with 17 cases in 1999.

The record is not as good with pertussis. Fear of bad effects of the vaccine and ignorance of the disease has caused a persistence of whooping cough particularly in young adults. There were 3249 cases in 1999.

Measles. mumps and rubella (MMR) are down to a few hundred cases each year.

Hemophilus influenza meningitis has almost disappeared from Pediatric Wards. For many years I saw many children with that form of meningitis and now there are only several hundred cases each year.

Hepatitis B and Hepatitis A vaccines are now part of routine childhood immunizations.

Varicella (Chicken Pox) Vaccine is available but is not as universally used as it should be. Varicella is regarded as a mild disease but 100 children still die from it each year.

The great improvement in the quality of the lives of children in the last 50 years has come from the use of the immunizations that have become available to prevent disease.

When I arrived in South Bend in 1950, children were still becoming ill with whooping cough. In the United States, 6000 children died with Pertussis each year. After the Pertussis vaccine was available, there was a great decrease in that disease.

Although tetanus vaccine was available, I would have to treat 2-3 children with that disease each year. The last patient I saw with tetanus was a 3-year old girl who had been burned. She was wrapped in a horse blanket to put out the fire. She was the last patient that I had with lockjaw and that was 30 years ago.

Twelve children from migrant families in Michigan City came down with Diphtheria in the 1950s. I have not seen this disease since.

We now have vaccines that protect our children against Diphtheria, Pertussis, Tetanus (DPT); Measles, Mumps, Rubella (MMR); Poliomyelitis, H. Influenza meningitis. Hepatitis A, Hepatitis B and Chicken Pox.

All of this has happened in my medical life- time. To me it is a miracle to be able to prevent diseases that before would cause serious illness or death.

Freedom from these diseases allows our children to have life and live it more abundantly.

Life expectancy has improved from 49.2 years in 1900 to 76.5 years in 2000. This is an increase in the expected life span of over 27 years in the past century. If this same trend continues, people may have a life expectancy of over 103 years by the end of this century.

These improvements are the result of a number of factors. In 1915, 100 infants per 1000 live births died in the first year of life. In 1938, the infant mortality rate was down to 7 deaths per 1000 live births.

After the first year of life there were still many hazards. During the first years of the 20th century, the leading causes of child deaths were diarrhea, diphtheria, measles, pneumonia, influenza, scarlet fever, tuberculosis, typhoid fever and whooping cough.

Immunizations, antibiotics and improved sanitation have almost completely eliminated these diseases as the causes of childhood deaths.

Injuries and deaths did occur on family farms and in factories were young children were workers.

What are the leading causes of death in the United States today and what can we do about them?

Heart disease, cancer, stroke, COPD (chronic obstructive respiratory disease), accidents, pneumonia, influenza, diabetes, suicide, kidney disease and liver disease are the causes of death which today's children will face as they grow older.

A vaccine is now available which can be given to infants and children to prevent ear infections, pneumonia and meningitis caused by pneumococcal disease. A different Pneumococcus vaccine is available for older adults to prevent certain types of pneumonia. Influenza vaccine is available to try to prevent influenza. Immunizations against Hepatitis A and against Hepatitis B are available.

Tests can be done to determine if a child will develop diabetes. Proper diet or other measures may delay or prevent the development of diabetes. Testing is most important in a family where a member has diabetes.

HOW CAN WE IMPROVE CHILDREN'S HEALTH?

We should be happy with the many ways which we have learned to prevent disease and disability in our children but we are failing in several areas.

The $15 million anti-smoking project involving 8,377 school children in Seattle, Washington was a failure. After 14 years a program designed to instruct children how to resist tobacco use has been stopped. A curriculum for grades 3-10 was designed by experts at the National Cancer Institute and taught by trained teachers. The study started in September 1984 and continued until September 1999. Surveys showed that 25% of the children in the study were daily smokers by the 12th grade. That rate of smoking was identical to the rate in children who were not in the study.

Smoking is linked to 8 types of cancer and to heart and lung disease.

In 2001, 27% of the people in the United States are obese compared to 23% in 1990 and 15% in 1970. Obese does not mean a few pounds over- weight. Obesity is defined as 30# or more over a normal body weight.

Being overweight increases the individual's change of developing heart disease, high blood pressure or diabetes. As children and adults sit more in front of TV screens and have more food served to them, more of them will become obese.

Another problem lifestyle area is the need to convince teenagers that drinking alcohol and driving a car is not a good mixture.

All children need to have the knowledge that will allow them to become architects of their own health. Children receive information from their parents and from their school teachers. Children also receive good and bad information from television programs.

It is very important that the health facts that children receive are accurate and timely. To assist parents and teachers, Memorial Hospital opened the HealthWorks! Kids' Museum one year ago on February 12, 2000. Since then, over 25,000 children have visited the center and participated in 1000 interactive learning classes and exhibits.

The purpose of HealthWorks is to provide medical information in a fun way so that children may make intelligent healthful decisions about their lifestyle.

Today's children have the potential to live for 100 years. Memorial Hospital's HealthWorks! Kids' Museum is dedicated to helping children live all those years in good health to become tomorrow's healthy, fulfilled adults.

Every child needs two parents.

The South Bend Clinic & SurgiCenter 211 N. Eddy at LaSalle, P.O. Box 1755, South Bend, IN 46634   Phone 219/234-8161

ALLERGY AND CLINICAL IMMUNOLOGY
ROBERT W. CLAUSEN, M.D.
JAMES B. HARRIS III, M.D.

DERMATOLOGY
HOLLY L. HAKE HARRIS, M.D.
CYNTHIA E. MAYFIELD, M.D.

ENDOCRINOLOGY – DIABETES
ELDRED H. MacDONELL, M.D.
JOHN J. CAVANAUGH, M.D.

FACIAL PLASTIC SURGERY
DAVID A. CAMPBELL, M.D.

FAMILY PRACTICE –
GRANGER FAMILY MEDICINE
JOSEPH H. CERBIN, M.D.
S. JESSE HSIEH, M.D.

GASTROENTEROLOGY
OLIVER D. GILLIAM, M.D.

GENERAL AND VASCULAR SURGERY
RANDOLPH E. SZLABICK, M.D.
JOHN W. SCHURZ, M.D.

INTERNAL MEDICINE
NELS R. LEININGER, M.D.
GAIL A. ENGLISH, M.D.
MICHAEL A. STRZELECKI, M.D.
THOMAS P. BARBOUR, M.D.
NINA S. BARBOUR, M.D.
MARK S. STANISH, M.D.

NEUROLOGY
P. JUSTIN KEENAN, M.D.

OBSTETRICS AND GYNECOLOGY
NANCY KELLER MADDEN, M.D.
SARA C. STRICKLER, M.D.
KAREY JO HOGUE, O.G.N.P.

OPHTHALMOLOGY
KAZIMIR J. ODRCIC, M.D.
MARTYN A. WILLS, M.D.
DAVID M. IVEY, M.D.

ORTHOPAEDIC SURGERY
Z.W. SOBOL, M.D.
FREDERICK D. RAU, M.D.

OTOLARYNGOLOGY
(EAR-NOSE-THROAT)
DAVID M. SABATO, M.D.
DAVID A. CAMPBELL, M.D.
LUKE P. PHILIPPSEN, M.D.

PEDIATRICS
G. WALTER ERICKSON, M.D.
GEORGE A. HORVATH, M.D.
TIMOTHY J. DURHAM, M.D.
JILL O. NOREUIL, M.D.
JAN E. SANDERS, M.D.

RHEUMATOLOGY
ALAN J. BIRNBAUM, M.D.

UROLOGY
RICHARD J. HOLLOWAY, M.D.

AUDIOLOGY
MARY E. DILLON, M.S.

ROENTGENOLOGY
RADIOLOGY, INC.

ADMINISTRATOR
EUGENE LADEWSKI

CHIEF FINANCIAL OFFICER
RICHARD F. KLEE, JR., CPA

CHIEF OPERATING OFFICER
TERESA ROBERTS

December 15, 1991

To My Patients,
  and to the Parents and Grandparents of my Patients:

This is to inform you that I will be retiring from the practice of pediatrics after 50 years of being a pediatrician. It is not easy to retire and leave behind so many wonderful parents and children whom I have watched grow during these many years. I will be retiring about January 1, 1992. I will still be covering some weekends and evenings, but I will not be seeing my regular patients during any regular office hours.

I would recommend that any of you who wish would transfer to one of the other pediatricians at The South Bend Clinic. Your records are here, and if there is any information, specifically, that you want me to give one of your new doctors, I will be happy to do so. Most of you have already seen either Dr. George Horvath, Dr. Timothy Durham, Dr. Jill Noreuil, or Dr. Jan Sanders at one time or another. Please select the doctor of your choice.

It has been a privilege and an honor to have assisted with the care of your children. I appreciate the trust you have placed in me in allowing me to do so.

For some people, retirement may be easy. For a pediatrician, retirement is very difficult. I remember all the phone calls, the office visits, the house calls, the newborns, the patients in the hospitals, and the emergencies in the middle of the nights.

How do you say goodbye to thousands of children and their parents who have been almost your whole life for 50 years? -- with great difficulty, and maybe with a few tears.

With love,

G. Walter Erickson

G. Walter Erickson, M. D.

"At times the dead are closer to us than the living and the care and affection of the past stretch blessing hands over our lives, projecting a guardian care out of the shadows and helping us over hard places. There are certain kinds of love that few but the very wise fully understand until they have become memories."

Author Unknown